From Children's Literature to Readers Theatre

ALA Editions purchases fund advocacy, awareness, and accreditation programs for library professionals worldwide.

From Children's Literature to Readers Theatre

Elizabeth A. Poe

An imprint of the American Library Association
Chicago | 2013

Elizabeth A. Poe is a retired professor of children's and young adult literature who holds a PhD in Curriculum and Instruction from the University of Colorado at Boulder. She has also taught at the preschool, middle school, and high school levels. For the past ten years, she has organized Readers Theatre performances with authors at professional conferences across the US and around the world. She is a member of the 2014 Newbery Committee and has served on the Caldecott Committee and chaired the USBBY Outstanding International Books Committee, the Colorado Blue Spruce Young Adult Book Award, and the IRA Young Adult Choices project. She served as president of ALAN, editor of the *Journal of Children's Literature* and *The SIGNAL Journal,* and book review column editor for *The ALAN Review.* A frequent speaker at professional conferences, she has published numerous journal articles and book chapters. Her other books are *Focus on Sexuality: A Reference Handbook, Focus on Relationships: A Reference Handbook,* and *Presenting Barbara Wersba.*

Printed in the United States of America
17 16 15 14 13   5 4 3 2 1

Extensive effort has gone into ensuring the reliability of the information in this book; however, the publisher makes no warranty, express or implied, with respect to the material contained herein.

ISBNs: 978-0-8389-1049-8 (paper); 978-0-8389-9640-9 (PDF). For more information on digital formats, visit the ALA Store at alastore.ala.org and select eEditions.

Library of Congress Cataloging-in-Publication Data

Poe, Elizabeth Ann.
    From children's literature to readers theatre / Elizabeth A. Poe.
        pages cm
    Includes bibliographical references and index.
    ISBN 978-0-8389-1049-8
    1. Children's libraries—Activity programs. 2. Young adults' libraries—Activity programs. 3. Readers' theater. 4. Drama in education. I. Title.
    Z718.3.P64 2013
    027.62'5—dc23   2012027258

Cover design by Kirstin Krutsch. Images © Shutterstock, Inc.

Book design by Kimberly Thornton in Charis SIL, ITC American Typewriter, and Proxima Nova.

♾ This paper meets the requirements of ANSI/NISO Z39.48-1992 (Permanence of Paper).

To Ruth Cline
Professor, Mentor, Friend

Contents

Part II: A How-To Guide

Foreword

by Katherine Paterson
National Ambassador for Young People's Literature

READERS THEATRE HAS ALL SORTS OF BENEFITS FOR THE PARTICIPANTS, and Elizabeth Poe's book is going to tell you about them in detail, but for me the most important thing about Readers Theatre is that it is great fun. Some years ago, four of us were doing a version of Brian Selznik's *The Invention of Hugo Cabret,* and Brian had written in all these sound effects we were to do that had to be carefully choreographed to work. The more we tried, the worse we seemed to get until the four of us collapsed in giggles. But practice, as you will learn when you read this book, is part of the fun, and by performance time, we were, if not perfect, impressive enough to wow our audience.

Surprises are another part of the fun. Elizabeth and I decided that we should take Readers Theatre not only on the road, but across the sea. At the World Congress of the International Board for Young People's Literature in Capetown, we planned a program using books and authors from the United States and South Africa. The other American author had to cancel at the last minute, so the South African coordinator found us a substitute. A former radio actor, he proved to be a wonderful addition. As I said later to our missing American, "Well, we missed you, but let's face it you probably can't burp like an elephant." The ability to burp on cue proved to be a secret talent of our South African substitute, which he used in a folk-tale about a greedy elephant, giving an elephant-sized burp after ingesting each unfortunate victim.

Getting to know your fellow readers in a new way is another part of the fun. Even in situations where children or teens think they know each other well, they will come to know each other better and appreciate each other more through the process of working together to develop a script, rehearsing it, and performing it.

If you think all this would be more efficient and better done by a teacher or librarian in charge, please read this book and think again. Dr. Poe will help you understand just why this reader-centered approach will benefit everyone who takes part and be great fun as well.

Whenever I have done Readers Theatre with Elizabeth, she has explained to the teachers and librarians in the audience how they can translate what they have seen us do to what can happen in their own classrooms or libraries. When they ask if they can have copies of our scripts, she helps them see the value of the children or teens developing their own scripts from books they have read and enjoyed. You may not have been fortunate enough to hear her speak about Readers Theatre, but this book will make you feel that you have. Please read it, share its ideas with young people and, above all, have fun doing so.

Acknowledgments

I WOULD LIKE TO THANK EACH OF THE AUTHORS WHO ACCEPTED MY INVI-tation to participate in a Readers Theatre performance. Working with pros is always an amazing experience. Many of them continue to be involved via their boxed comments in each chapter. I see them as a sort of Greek chorus, adding their voices to the Readers Theatre story told herein. I am grateful to the publishers who generously sponsored these authors' partici-pation at professional conferences. I am also indebted to all the publishers who have sent me review copies over the past thirty-plus years. Having a wealth of quality literature at my fingertips helped me choose which au-thors to invite as well as which books to include in my chapter "Books to Consider: One Hundred Titles That Would Make Good Readers Theatre" (chapter 8). I offer my thanks as well to the teachers, librarians, and stu-dents with whom I have shared Readers Theatre experiences. I continue to learn from all of you. Finally, I express heartfelt appreciation to my editor, Stephanie Zvirin, for her incredible patience and expertise.

Part I

About Readers Theatre

Introducing Readers Theatre

Definition and Background of Readers Theatre

FIVE SECOND GRADERS STAND BEFORE A GROUP OF TWENTY PRESCHOOL children sitting on the rug in the library's story area. Each of them is holding a hardback copy of Eric Rohmann's picture book, *A Kitten Tale.*[1]

After the name and author of the book have been announced, the children begin to read as follows:

A (Nar):	Once there were four kittens who had never seen snow.
B (1ˢᵗ Kitten):	Snow scares me!
A (Nar):	Said the first kitten.
B (1ˢᵗ Kitten):	When winter comes, the snow will fall and fall and we'll all be cold!
C (2ⁿᵈ Kitten):	Freezing cold!
A (Nar):	Said the second kitten.
D (3ʳᵈ Kitten):	Cold to the tips of our tails!
A (Nar):	Said the third kitten. The fourth kitten said,
E (4ᵗʰ Kitten):	I can't wait.

The second graders continue through the book, reading their designated parts (indicated above by A, B, C, D, E). When they finish, they bow and sit down on the rug. The preschoolers clap enthusiastically and rush to the older children, wanting to see the pictures in the books they hold. The teachers and librarian, used to channeling the children's energy and curiosity, quickly organize the children into five small groups, with a second grader in each. The second graders agree to read the books with the children as they look at the pictures and discuss the story.

Comments like "Oh, the fourth kitten is striped like my cat at home"; "I love it when it snows"; "I was afraid to swim in the ocean until my mother went in with me last summer"; and "We have new kittens at our house!" fill the room. Several preschoolers pretend to be kittens, and soon one group is acting out *A Kitten Tale.* They particularly love shouting, "I can't wait," and pretending to roll in the snow.

In this room abuzz with literature-inspired conversation and dramatic play, the librarian and teachers look at one another and smile. The Readers Theatre performance has clearly been a success. The preschoolers' energetic response to the initial reading and their subsequent interest in hearing the book read repeatedly, drawing pictures of the four kittens, and eventually putting on *A Kitten Tale* puppet show all speak to the power of hearing older children give a Readers Theatre performance.

But the preschool audience members are not the only ones to benefit from the performance. (Indeed, it could be argued that they could have had a similarly positive experience in any well-executed storytime given by an adult interested in their reactions and comments.) The second graders, who participated in the project from inception to execution, experienced a variety of personal, social, and intellectual gains. They had fun working together to prepare the performance, and they had fun reading to and interacting with the preschoolers. They developed literary appreciation for a masterfully written and illustrated picture book. They improved their reading fluency and public speaking skills. And, in addition to experiencing the satisfaction that comes from helping others, they felt increased self-confidence by virtue of doing something well.

But all these benefits did not occur without a lot of hard work by the readers who volunteered for the project and the adults who wanted to help children develop a love for literature. The adults in this scenario care deeply about nurturing and empowering children. Helping children create a Readers Theatre in the library is one way to do so.

As the opening scenario demonstrates, Readers Theatre is a staged reading of literature that emphasizes the importance of text by using limited action, suggested characterization, no costumes, and no props. Sometimes called minimalist theatre, it is a dramatic form, originally developed for performing in theatrical settings, in which participants read from scripts taken directly from a literary work.

Educators have embraced this dramatic form for its myriad educational benefits and adapted it for a variety of purposes. Many teachers and reading specialists, who regard it as a tool for teaching reading skills, have students read from prefabricated scripts. This activity is widely lauded as an effective means for increasing reading fluency as students practice reading aloud with others for the sake of a performance. It can also familiarize students with a literary text and deepen their comprehension of the text because reading aloud successfully generally involves understanding what one is reading. It follows that understanding the text can help students read expressively. Educators with these goals in mind frequently rely upon the array of commercially produced scripts available to them.

Language arts teachers may have additional reasons for using Readers Theatre in libraries and classrooms. They may seek to deepen students' literary experience with a book, encourage language appreciation, provide a means for sharing books read in small groups, or offer an option for a group response to a book. These educators achieve their goals by encouraging students to create their own Readers Theatre scripts.

> I make picture books: words and images combined in a page-to-page format which tells a story. For me, these books are never silent. The words are meant to be read aloud while the pictures always provoke the other senses. But still I never really considered how a book like *A Kitten Tale* would sound spoken by many voices. So I gave it a go and now that I've been a kitten this is what I know: as a writer/illustrator I put my work into the world, but it is the reader who picks it up, looks it over and makes it his or her own. This happens every day with picture books: a parent reads the story at bedtime, or a teacher gathers her class and changes her voice to represent each kitten . . . and then maybe, the kids will ask to become the kittens and take the parts and transform the story into something different—something personal that tells us a story. The story becomes the point of departure for their expansive imaginations. What a wondrous thing to make something that kids, through their own creativity, turn into their own. —*Eric Rohmann*

While my approach to Readers Theatre encompasses the goals of both reading and language arts teachers, it stresses the use of reader-created scripts. When readers create and perform their own scripts, they not only improve their reading skills, but they also enhance their literary appreciation, thereby increasing their chances for developing a love of literature and becoming lifelong readers. I base this statement on John Dewey's philosophy of experiential education, Louise Rosenblatt's theory of reader response, and my thirty-plus years of experience as an educator.

According to John Dewey, learning takes place most profoundly when children are involved in the creation of the learning experience.[2] In our opening scenario, the children were highly involved in all stages of their Readers Theatre production. They first volunteered to be part of the project. Then they spent several afternoons perusing a stack of picture books suggested by the librarian. They talked with the preschool teachers about what the children might enjoy. After conferring with one another, they selected the book they wanted to use.

The next step was to prepare the script. They read and reread the story. Because there were six of them, the children decided that four would be the kittens, one would be the narrator (a term the librarian supplied for the person who would say everything the kittens didn't), and one would be the director (another term supplied by the librarian when the children quickly recognized that someone needed to be in charge). At the librarian's urging, they discussed whether the words told the story without the pictures. After deciding they did in all but one instance, the children collaborated to compose the additional words to insert into the script. The librarian helped the director type the script on the computer with reading roles labeled A, B, C, D, E. They glued each reader's parts to large sticky notes that they stuck over the original text on the appropriate pages of the books.

The director assigned parts, and the practicing began. The group rehearsed several afternoons until each member felt confident reading his or her part. During the practices, they discussed the kittens' different personalities and how those differences might affect the way their words were read. They practiced reading expressively, using consistent voices for each character. The librarian suggested a bit of work on rhythm and pacing. The director wrote a letter to the preschool class inviting them to a special storytime at the library.

The performance was a success, and it inspired the preschoolers to become involved in their own learning and love of books. The possible gains for the second graders are numerous. Certainly they improved their reading skills, but they went beyond that to increase their understanding of and appreciation for literature. Their work selecting the text meant they had to read many books closely and choose one suited for the audience. This required careful consideration of the books' subject matter and use of language. Writing the script, in this situation, did not necessitate making many changes. There was only one place where they had to imitate the writer's style to invent a line for the narrator to read when the text did not explain that the fourth kitten leaped out into the snow while the other kittens hid in the house. They did, however, come away with an important understanding concerning the relationship between illustrations and text in picture books. They also learned the term *narrator* and how this literary device functions in literature. They gained a sense of characterization as they delved into the personalities of the four kittens. In addition, they experienced firsthand the exhilarating effect sharing a good book can have on a group of listeners. In one way or another, each of the children involved in this project had a rich, satisfying experience with a literary text.

" I often work alone. It's just me, my camera, my imagination, and my computer. Readers Theatre was very different for me because it enables authors to work together as a group. I've never worked this way before. It was a very positive experience, and I learned a lot. For the first time I was able to really "feel" the words on the pages of another book and be present in the story without the props (i.e., illustrations).

I've already visited a school since I returned to England from Washington, D.C., and I used what I learned from my Readers Theatre experience in my workshop. The children enjoyed it a lot! —*Ifeoma Onyefulu*

Building on Dewey's philosophy of experiential education, which deals with learning in general, Louise Rosenblatt developed a theory of reader response primarily concerned with the nature of literary experiences.[3] According to Rosenblatt, every literary experience involves a reader, who comes to the printed word, or the text, with a unique set of characteristics, or experiences, which creates a transaction resulting in the reader's evocation of meaning from the text.[4] Because we are all individuals, each reader's response to a text is unique, its meaning special to him or her.

In the case of *A Kitten Tale,* several readers had different interpretations of the kittens' personalities, and that influenced how they thought a particular kitten's lines should be read. Different interpretations were respected, even celebrated, but group negotiations were needed to ensure the integrity of the performance. The children decided that each reader could read his or her kitten's lines the way he or she wanted as long as the voice was consistent and the kittens sounded different from one another. Negotiations such as these are an important part of learning to express one's response to a literary work, developing necessary collaboration skills, and understanding the process of creating a successful Readers Theatre experience. The audience's responses were also considered as the second graders talked with the preschoolers about how the book related to them and the teachers nurtured their desire to act out, draw, and perform their own responses to the story.

> " I loved participating in Readers Theatre with Linda Sue Park, Eric Rohmann, and M.T. Anderson and reading from each other's books. I had read and loved all their books previously, but taking a role and speaking the words gave me new insight and admiration for the books. I came away from our Readers Theatre experience feeling as if I had lived those books. The rehearsals were as much fun as the performance, and it was so easy to put on since we didn't have to memorize or use props or blocking. —*Shannon Hale*

As a teacher educator and children's/young adult literature specialist, I advocate using this child-centered approach to Readers Theatre as a pleasurable way of sharing stories that has a wealth of secondary benefits. I used it for many years in my university children's literature, young adult literature, and teaching methods courses. My hope is that when preservice teachers and librarians actually participate in a Readers Theatre experience, they will be more likely to use this activity in their own classrooms and libraries. It has been my pleasure to observe numerous reader-created Readers Theatre performances given by students of all educational levels in a variety of venues, both inside and outside of school settings. Students and adults have also given Readers Theatre demonstrations in conjunction with sessions I have conducted at professional conferences.

For the past ten years, I have been working with groups of children's authors giving Readers Theatre performances at professional conferences.

I have organized Readers Theatre sessions at national conferences in Florida, Nevada, Texas, Illinois, Washington, D.C., and California as well as at international conferences in South Africa, Denmark, and Spain. I work with a different group of authors each time I do this, so each performance is a fresh experience. The sessions given at ALA Annual Conferences in Washington, D.C., and Anaheim, California, were particularly rewarding to me because the librarians seemed deeply interested in organizing opportunities for children and teens to create Readers Theatre experiences in their libraries. They asked excellent questions that I was unable to answer as fully as I would have liked. These librarians are the inspiration for this book.

I firmly believe the library to be a perfect setting for children and teens to encounter Readers Theatre, whether as reading participants or audience members. I am eager to pass on insights gained from the students, authors, and colleagues with whom I have worked and from whom I have learned. Many of the examples I give are taken directly from my work with children's authors. Because they are participating in Readers Theatre for the first time, they are not unlike the children in our libraries and classrooms—and it is interesting to hear from and about the people who write books we love. Other examples come from the children, teens, or colleagues with whom I have shared Readers Theatre experiences. Some examples are composites; others are scenarios I created based on my experiences, both positive and negative, with Readers Theatre performances. In all cases, they are included with the goal of answering questions raised by librarians and teachers, thereby enabling children and teens to create their own joyful Readers Theatre experiences.

Notes

1. Eric Rohmann, *A Kitten Tale* (New York: Knopf, 2008).
2. John Dewey, *Experience and Education* (New York: Colliers, 1938).
3. Louise M. Rosenblatt, *Literature as Exploration* (New York: Appleton-Century, 1938).
4. Elizabeth Ann Poe, "Reader Responses of Pregnant Adolescents and Teenage Mothers to Young Adult Novels Portraying Protagonists with Problems Similar and Dissimilar to the Readers'" (unpublished dissertation, University of Colorado, 1986).

2

Collaboration
Is Key

The Value of the Collaborative
Reader-Centered Model

━━━━━━━━━━━━━━━━━━━━━━━━━━━━━

HAVING TOUCHED ON SOME OF THE BENEFITS OF GIVING A READERS THE-atre performance and creating Readers Theatre scripts in chapter 1, I would like to emphasize here that collaboration is key to a successful reader-centered Readers Theatre experience. Effective collaboration can augment the social, personal, and intellectual gains of Readers Theatre participants as well as enhance the presentation itself.

I base this statement on my experiences observing top-down Readers Theatre models and developing my own collaborative reader-centered ap-proach. In a top-down model, someone in a position of authority hands the script to the readers and directs their reading of it. The script may have been purchased or developed by someone who is not one of the readers. While a top-down Readers Theatre performance may indeed be deemed successful by the audience, this approach emphasizes the *theatre* rather than the *reader* in Readers Theatre. The collaborative approach I advocate is reader-centered. Involving the readers in all aspects of the production increases opportunities for gains on many levels.

Of course there are degrees of collaboration and reader-centeredness, but a group that closely met my ideals was the ALA Readers Theatre that performed at the organization's 2008 Annual Conference in Anaheim, California. Our author-readers were M. T. (Tobin) Anderson, Shannon Hale, Linda Sue Park, and Eric Rohmann. From the onset, this group engaged in a congenial collaboration that made working with them a pleasurable and noteworthy experience. Their actions, experiences, and comments provide interesting examples regarding the potential social, personal, and intellectual ramifications of Readers Theatre.

A library-based Readers Theatre can be viewed as a social situation in which children and teens take part voluntarily for fun. Everything else is secondary. Of course there are many reasons for giving a Readers Theatre performance, but first and foremost, it should be an enjoyable experience involving other people. When the 2008 ALA group was practicing, there was so much laughter and goofing around that someone passing by our practice room could have thought it was purely a social gathering, not a rehearsal for a performance to be given before six hundred people. In the question-and-answer session following the performance, one librarian asked about children getting off task. We all laughed.

Tobin Anderson quickly responded that this group had spent twelve hours together in preparation for the performance, and three-fourths of that was spent socializing—talking about families and friends, eating, comparing writing routines, eating, discussing each other's books, eating, making jokes, eating, discussing books they had read, eating, comparing religious beliefs, eating, and thinking up outrageous ways to perform Readers Theatre. All this "off-task" behavior is not only fun, it also helps groups work together. It helps group members bond, and it raises members' comfort levels.

When members can relax and feel part of the group, they are more apt to engage in the social cooperation needed to complete the tasks at hand: collaborating to select texts, converting them to scripts, practicing, and performing. In addition, working in collaboration can help develop important social skills, such as the negotiating described in chapter 1. It can also afford opportunities to share related or off-topic ideas with others. I have heard authors give each other helpful advice about dealing with editors and publishers. Likewise, discussing parents, siblings, teachers, or other off-topic subjects with each other can prove helpful to children and teens involved with Readers Theatre. Along with its social aspects, collaborative work can lead to a variety of personal gains.

On a personal level, working in a Readers Theatre can be a rewarding experience just because it is great fun. The 2008 ALA group demonstrated what pure pleasure it can be to work with one's peers. I know the positive peer relationships they established as a group have grown into friendships. Each time I see one of them at a conference, I get an unsolicited report on who has visited whom, and so on. Virginia Euwer Wolff so appreciated the support from her peers in the 2007 ALA Readers Theatre troupe that she thanks her Readers Theatre colleagues David Almond, Cornelia Funke, Tim Wynne-Jones, and Elizabeth Poe in the acknowledgments to *This Full House*. Positive peer interactions can also occur when children and teens are engaged in Readers Theatre, and friendships frequently develop from these connections. Additionally, working on a Readers Theatre may enable children and teens to develop positive relationships with librarians, teachers, parents, volunteers, or other caring adults helping with the project.

> " By participating in Readers Theatre, I learned so much about the books—including and especially my own. From writing the script to rehearsing with the other authors then performing in front of an enthusiastic audience. . . . at every step my exploration and understanding of the texts deepened. What a gift to be able to experience my stories and those of the other authors in such a new and enlightening way.
> —*Linda Sue Park*

As mentioned before, reading skills of all types can be practiced throughout the process of developing a Readers Theatre. This applies to adults as well as children. Over the years, I have had several authors tell me that participating in Readers Theatre helped them give public readings of their work. One was even inspired to accept an ALA Poetry Slam invitation due to his positive experience with Readers Theatre. A positive experience as a child or teen can help overcome performance fears. A positive Readers Theatre performance can also show children and teens that working hard and doing something well can be deeply satisfying. Recognition from family and peers can be exceptionally rewarding. But above all, a positive Readers Theatre experience can be a step toward developing a lifelong love of literature.

Literary appreciation can improve the quality of one's life. While many librarians, educators, and other adults might agree with this statement, it is a difficult concept to impart to children and teens. In fact, we should not even try to do this directly. It is better to do it indirectly by creating pleasurable experiences with literature for young people. Readers Theatre has the potential to be one such experience.

Many young people, particularly teens, resent being told what they have to read. Therefore, offering them the opportunity to choose what they will read is important if they are to have an enjoyable experience. Sometimes the purpose of the performance dictates certain limitations, but no matter the parameters, some type of choice is usually possible. Ideally, the selection of the literary work or works will afford the opportunity to read widely with a particular intention in mind.

For example, conducting an author study or preparing for an author visit would require participants to read a wide array of works by one author. The process here is similar to the one I use when I work with authors and ask them to choose which of their own works they would like the group to perform. If the performance is to coincide with a holiday or address a specific topic or theme, readers can explore related books and then choose what they want to perform. If the purpose of the performance is to provide cross-cultural and international literary experiences, the readers' perusal of literary works would be shaped accordingly.

Throughout the selection process, librarians or teachers may want to suggest books to be considered. Reading to select the texts can expose participants to a variety of books, and thus nudge readers toward quality literature they might enjoy. Collaborating to select the Readers Theatre texts can also be fun and literarily enlightening for group members.

In addition to selecting the texts, participants must also choose the passages that will be used. The close reading required first to identify the passage to be read and then to convert it into a

> I really enjoyed working with Elizabeth Poe on Readers Theatre. It's a lovely, creative way of opening up a book that helps to draw out layers of meaning and emotion. It's great to dramatise in this way, to stress the importance of sound, rhythm, pacing, voice, and gesture, which are so crucial to all writing and reading. It's also great fun!
>
> —David Almond

script deepens the child's or teen's literary experience with that work. It provides a window into the author's artistry that can enhance understanding of plot structure; provide insight into character development; increase awareness of voice, diction, and dialogue; inspire engagement with theme; and create awareness of subtle nuances. Looking at these literary characteristics for the authentic purpose of creating a script that will convey accurately the author's work can enhance the reader's relationship with that work. If any of this can be achieved without using a didactic approach, Readers Theatre participants may well derive deeper aesthetic pleasure from reading quality literature.

Closely related to the intellectual aspects of literary analysis is the ability to match a book to an audience. Because this complex cognitive skill involves looking at a piece of literature from another's perspective, the reader must understand not only the text, but other people as well and anticipate how they might respond to the literary work. Other intellectual benefits of Readers Theatre participation include gaining insights into how groups function, improving organizational skills, and increasing understanding of the dramatic form called Readers Theatre. All these can be achieved indirectly through participation and reflection.

Of course the social, personal, and intellectual aspects of a Readers Theatre experience overlap, and individual participants will experience only some of the advantages they offer. But taken as a whole, Readers Theatre illustrates the exciting potential of the collaborative reader-centered model.

Resources

Dewey, John. *Experience and Education.* New York: Colliers, 1938.

Poe, Elizabeth Ann. "Reader Responses of Pregnant Adolescents and Teenage Mothers to Young Adult Novels Portraying Protagonists with Problems Similar and Dissimilar to the Readers'." Unpublished dissertation. University of Colorado, 1986.

Rohmann, Eric. *A Kitten Tale.* New York: Knopf, 2008.

Rosenblatt, Louise M. *Literature as Exploration.* New York: Appleton-Century, 1938.

Wolff, Virginia Euwer. *This Full House.* New York: The Bowen Press/Harper Teen, 2009.

Exploring a Wealth of Possibilities

Ways to Use Readers Theatre in Library Settings

NAOMI SHIHAB NYE SITS MESMERIZED, INTENT ON THE WORDS READ BY four college students. When they finish, she wipes a tear from her eye and applauds enthusiastically. Later, she thanks the students for treating her words so kindly and tells her audience how moving it was to hear a passage from her novel *Habibi* transformed into a Readers Theatre presentation. Nye is a featured author at the West Virginia Book Festival, and the preservice teachers and librarians giving the performance are students at West Virginia University. The purpose for their performance is to introduce Nye by way of one of her young adult novels.

Although this introduction was given by university students studying Nye's works in my young adult literature course, it could well have been prepared and presented by middle or high school students from a local school or public library. Authors frequently speak at local and state conferences, libraries, schools, and bookstores. A librarian who volunteered to help organize a Readers Theatre introduction would be performing a service not only for the organization, institution, or business involved, but for the children or teen participants as well. I know these university students will never forget how gratifying it was to have Naomi Shihab Nye praise them publicly and privately for the quality of their work.

Similarly, children and teens can give Readers Theatre presentations as gifts to authors who visit their schools or libraries. The sixth-grade students at Blacksburg Middle School in Virginia did this for Carolyn Meyer when she attended a potluck dinner given in her honor. The Readers Theatre performance of *Where the Broken Heart Still Beats,* among one of the many group projects prepared in response to her books, touched her deeply. The other sixth graders, their family members, and special guests enjoyed it as well.

At the college level, a group of my young adult literature students gave a Readers Theatre performance of *The Captive* for Joyce Hansen when she visited our class at Radford University. Another group gave a Readers Theatre performance of *Grandma's Records* for Eric Velasquez when he spoke at our language arts teaching methods class at West Virginia University. In both cases, the authors were visibly impressed by the students' rendering of their words, and told them so repeatedly.

In their written reflections on the experience, a few of the students said they had been anxious about performing for the author, but that it had proven to be a rewarding experience. Several mentioned that they would try to provide such opportunities for the children with whom they would work in the future. Clearly, the middle school and university students formed special relationships with these visiting authors. Again, these Readers Theatre performances and the subsequent positive interactions could just as well have involved groups of young library patrons and an author visiting the library to give a talk or book signing.

Thus far, the examples have involved authors watching their works performed, but this does not always need to be the case. There are many audiences that would benefit from and enjoy watching young people perform Readers Theatre. The following suggestions are ideally suited for school or public library settings.

As was illustrated in the opening scenario in chapter 1, Readers Theatre performances can give older children an opportunity to perform for younger children. In that situation, second graders performed for preschoolers. Taking advantage of the natural admiration younger children hold for older children, librarians can arrange for elementary school children to perform for kindergarteners, middle schoolers to perform for elementary children, high schoolers to perform for middle schoolers, and all the variations in between.

In cases such as these, where the audience is of the same age group, selecting the right work to perform entails knowing what readers of that age in general enjoy and what that particular group would like to hear. At a school library performance, older children may decide to read from books relating to topics younger students have been studying. For example, first graders learning about owls might readily engage with fourth graders performing Jane Yolen's *Owl Moon*. Sixth graders studying the western movement, on the other hand, might thoroughly enjoy hearing a series of excerpts from Theodore Taylor's *Walking Up a Rainbow* performed by eighth graders. And sophomores studying World War II might appreciate hearing Laurie Friedman's picture book *Angel Girl* or selections from titles such as Katherine Paterson's *Jacob Have I Loved,* Annika Thor's *A Faraway Island,* David Chotjewitz's *Daniel Half Human and the Good Nazi,* Eli Wiesel's *Night,* and Markus Zusak's *The Book Thief* performed by seniors.

Performances at public libraries are more likely to be given for mixed-age audiences comprising community members and performers' family and friends. In these cases, group members can choose from a wide range of approaches. They might decide that each of them will select a favorite book and prepare a script for the entire group. This would mean that the group would perform several unrelated pieces. I use this approach when working with groups of authors who give Readers Theatre presentations as part of professional conference sessions; the variety of selections is always fascinating.

Other approaches involve some sort of overarching concept. Participants may have a particular author, topic, or genre that they wish to present in a Readers Theatre performance. Over the years, I have seen students perform Readers Theatre based on the works of authors such as Kathryn Lasky, Robert McCloskey, Joyce Hansen, Avi, Will Hobbs, Carolyn Meyer, Lois Lowry, Cynthia Voigt, and Walter Dean Myers. I have also seen performances focused on topics such as friendship, unrequited love, the cycle of life, and First Amendment rights. Genre-based performances have included science fiction, fantasy, historical fiction, and contemporary realism. While these performances were generally given in classroom settings related to curricular requirements, young library patrons could also choose a favorite author, topic, or genre upon which to base a Readers Theatre performance.

Although open-ended situations give participants freedom to determine what they will perform, librarians sometimes have a particular topic or theme they wish participants to address. There may be a festival or a visiting author in town, for instance. But even when the purpose for the presentation is predetermined, it is important to offer volunteers opportunities to choose their own focus and literature.

For example, if the library wants to sponsor an Earth Day event, the librarian might help Readers Theatre volunteers brainstorm a focus by suggesting environmental issues such as global warming or rain forests as possible topics. He or she would help participants find appropriate literature by pointing them toward the growing body of literature on each of these topics. Julia Golding's eco-fantasy *The Companions Quartet,* Saci Lloyd's *The Carbon Diaries 2015,* Jennifer Cowan's novel *Earthgirl,* and Melanie Walsh's picture book *10 Things I Can Do to Help My World* all deal with global warming and environmental issues. Lynne Cherry's picture book *The Great Kapok Tree: A Tale of the Amazon Rain Forest* and Aileen Kilgore Henderson's middle-grade novel *The Monkey Thief,* which takes place in Costa Rica, would be good starting points for finding books on rain forests around the globe.

Alternatively, performers may decide to highlight one author for their Earth Day presentation by focusing on selected titles that address an issue such as endangered species. Because many of his books feature an endangered animal species, Will Hobbs would be a natural choice for

> **"** When Elizabeth Poe first approached me about Readers Theatre, I found myself harkening back to one of my English teachers in high school who liked to get us up on our feet reading aloud. Good, you say, and rightly so, but she limited this experience to Shakespeare, and, truth to tell, it was often excruciating. I remember vividly a shy mouse of a girl having to read the love scene from *Romeo and Juliet* with the school's new boy, for whom English was a second language. Considering that Shakespeare is already a second language for pretty well everybody, he was at a double disadvantage. The result was torture—for poor Romeo and his mousy beloved as well as the whole class!
>
> Readers Theatre, however, is something else, entirely, and I was immediately

such an event. *Changes in Latitudes* is about saving endangered sea turtles; *Beardance* focuses on rescuing an endangered grizzly bear cub; and *The Maze* deals with releasing fledgling endangered condors back into the wild. Highlighting his endangered species books can lead to awareness of Hobbs's other books or books on endangered species by other authors. Of course, the same potential expansion applies for any topic or theme selected by Readers Theatre performers.

Award lists offer another type of overarching construct for organizing Readers Theatre performances. Caldecott, Newbery, and Printz winners are an obvious place to start with this idea. As performers peruse books from these lists, they will quickly discover that some can be readily adapted as Readers Theatre scripts and others cannot. A performance using excerpts from four to six books could show the range of books receiving each of these awards. Listings of state book award nominees and winners can be used in a similar manner. If participants are interested in an international emphasis, the Outstanding International Books lists compiled by the United States Board on Books for Young People (USBBY) provide an array of titles first published outside the United States. On a similar note, Batchelder winners celebrate titles publishers have translated into English.

Translation raises some interesting possibilities concerning Readers Theatre. I first became aware of how translation enters into a Readers Theatre performance when I was working with the 2008 International Board on Books for Young People (IBBY) Readers Theatre troupe in Copenhagen, Denmark. The group was composed of two American authors, Katherine Paterson and Peter Sís, and two Danish authors, Lene Kaaberbøl and Louis Jensen. Although Readers Theatre performances can be given in any

---

drawn to it, hook, line, and sinker. The only thing better than being read to is being read to by a whole cast! I couldn't wait to give it a try, myself, with a group of young people. Luckily, I have access to a whole theatre school of them, courtesy of the Ottawa School of Speech and Drama. And so for the launch of my second Rex Zero book, *Rex Zero: King of Nothing*, instead of doing a reading myself, I chose two scenes from the book and divvied up the roles, with myself as one narrator and a sparky Rex look-alike as an alternate narrator. It was so much fun and so well received! With only two rehearsals, the kids did a bang-up job, although I'd have loved to have had two more rehearsals with them. They had a great time. I had a great time. *—Tim Wynne-Jones*

language, this presentation was to be in English. Jensen did not have any books translated into English, but he did have a manuscript of one of his novels that an acquaintance had translated. He developed his script from that. But when the script read awkwardly in rehearsals, Kaaberbøl, who was familiar with the original Danish version, pointed out that the translation was weak in many places and the beauty of Jensen's writing, for which he is famous in Denmark, was not coming through. Jensen took her comments seriously, we all worked at improving the translation, and I gained insight into another way to use Readers Theatre.

Readers Theatre presentations could be given by groups who translate texts from English into another language commonly spoken in a community. Because preparing and reading scripts demands such close attention to the author's words, those members of the group doing the original translation would deepen their understanding of the language in the original work. In addition, all group members would be in a position to give quality feedback based on their experience reading the translated script. Thus, a group of Hmong students studying English would benefit greatly from translating something like Robert McCloskey's *Make Way for Ducklings* into Hmong and performing it for young children and their families in both languages. Libraries that host English as second language classes might want to ask teens in the community to perform works in translation for English language learners of all ages.

Bilingual texts also offer rich possibilities for Readers Theatre performances. *Sopa de Frijoles/Bean Soup* by Jorge Argueta and *Delicious Hullabaloo/Pachanga deliciosa* by Pat Mora are picture books with Spanish and English versions of the text on each page. Readers could have lots of fun deciding how to mingle the two languages in a Readers Theatre presentation. They could read the passage from each first in one language and then the other; they could read the whole book in one language at a time; or they could alternate languages sentence by sentence. But however the readers choose to perform it, library patrons of all ages will enjoy and benefit from such a lively bilingual Readers Theatre presentation.

So far, I have suggested ways Readers Theatre could be used in library settings, but performances don't necessarily have to be given in libraries. Reader Theatre productions that have originated in libraries could be performed in preschools, hospitals, nursing homes, community centers, or other libraries. The same considerations regarding audience and literary selections apply no matter where the performance takes place. It is, however, important that new selections are made for each performance to avoid becoming stale and to remain appropriate for the situation. Fortunately, just as there is a wealth of possibilities for Readers Theatre performances, there is a wealth of literature to make fresh Readers Theatre performances a continued possibility.

See chapter 8 for a bibliography of one hundred titles that would make good Readers Theatre.

Resources

Argueta, Jorge. *Sopa de frijoles/Bean Soup: Un poema para cocinar/A Cooking Poem.* Illustrated by Rafael Yockteng. Toronto: Groundwood, 2009.

Cherry, Lynne. *The Great Kapok Tree: A Tale of the Amazon Rain Forest.* San Diego: Gulliver Green/Harcourt Brace, 1990.

Chotjewitz, David. *Daniel Half Human and the Good Nazi.* Translated by Doris Orgel. New York: Richard Jackson/Atheneum, 2004.

Cowan, Jennifer. *Earthgirl.* Toronto: Groundwood, 2009.

Friedman, Laurie. *Angel Girl: Based on a True Story.* Illustrated by Ofra Amit. Minneapolis: Carolrhoda, 2008.

Golding, Julia. *The Chimera's Curse.* Tarrytown, NY: Marshall Cavendish, 2008.

———. *The Gorgon's Gaze.* Tarrytown, NY: Marshall Cavendish, 2008.

———. *Mines of the Minotaur.* Tarrytown, NY: Marshall Cavendish, 2008.

———. *Secrets of the Sirens.* Tarrytown, NY: Marshall Cavendish, 2007.

Hansen, Joyce. *The Captive.* New York: Scholastic, 1994.

Henderson, Aileen Kilgore. *The Monkey Thief.* Minneapolis: Milkweed, 1997.

Hobbs, Will. *Beardance.* New York: Bradbury, 1993.

———. *Changes in Latitudes.* New York: Atheneum, 1988.

———. *The Maze.* New York: Morrow, 1998.

Lloyd, Saci. *The Carbon Diaries 2015.* New York: Holiday House, 2009.

McCloskey, Robert. *Make Way for Ducklings.* New York: Viking, 1941.

Meyer, Carolyn. *Where the Broken Heart Still Beats: The Story of Cynthia Ann Parker.* San Diego: Harcourt Brace, 1992.

Mora, Pat. *Delicious Hullabaloo/Pachanga deliciosa.* Illustrated by Francisco X. Mora. Spanish translation by Alba Nora Martínez and Pat Mora. Houston, TX: Pinata/Arte Público, 1998.

Nye, Naomi Shihab. *Habibi.* New York: Simon and Schuster, 1997.

Paterson, Katherine. *Jacob Have I Loved.* New York: Thomas Y. Crowell, 1980.

Taylor, Theodore. *Walking Up a Rainbow.* San Diego: Harcourt, 1986.

Thor, Annika. *A Faraway Island*. Translated by Linda Schenck. New York: Delacorte, 2009.

Velasquez, Eric. *Grandma's Records*. New York: Walker, 2001.

Walsh, Melanie. *10 Things I Can Do to Help My World*. New York: Candlewick, 2008.

Wiesel, Eli. *Night*. New York: Hill and Wang, 1972.

Yolen, Jane. *Owl Moon*. Illustrated by John Schoenherr. New York: Philomel, 1987.

Zusak, Markus. *The Book Thief*. New York: Knopf, 2006.

Setting the Stage

Steps for Creating Readers Theatre Experiences

A SUCCESSFUL READER-CENTERED READERS THEATRE EXPERIENCE RE-quires harmonious collaborations and thoughtful preparation. Teachers and librarians play crucial roles in creating rewarding experiences by providing the structure and assistance that enable each group to be as autonomous as possible. Of course the amount of structure or assistance needed will vary depending on the ages of participants and the purpose of the presentation. However, some general guidelines and processes apply to all who use a reader-centered approach to Readers Theatre.

I suggest adults working with Readers Theatre groups begin by reading these guidelines and then creating a Readers Theatre experience with their peers. Going through the steps themselves will deepen their understanding of the process and facilitate their decisions about how to adapt each step with different-aged children. Although this exercise will result in a model script and demonstration performance to help get participants started, I sincerely hope teachers and librarians will resist giving their adult-created scripts to children, a practice contrary to the reader-centered approach described below.

Forming the Group

The first step in creating a Readers Theatre experience is forming the group. When I work with groups of authors, I build the group by inviting authors one at a time. My goal is to bring together four writers of top-quality children's or young adult literature who can work together congenially to demonstrate a Readers Theatre performance to librarians and teachers at a professional conference. This very specific purpose requires forming a very specific group, so it is appropriate that it be by invitation only. But of course this would not be the case in most school or library settings. Readers Theatre groups in these situations will most likely be composed of people who have read or who will read the same books.

In the former case, students wanting to read the same book have been grouped in small literature circles of four to six people. The purpose of their Readers Theatre presentation might be to introduce the book to others in the class who have not read it or to family and friends in a community performance. In the latter case, the groups may be formed for the express purpose of giving a Readers Theatre performance in a library setting. These participants will most likely be responding to a general invitation asking for four to six volunteers who are interested in reading a variety of books and giving a Readers Theatre performance. It is a good idea if this general invitation specifies the age range of the volunteers and, if known, the audience for whom they will be performing.

Four to six people is a workable size group. If more children or teens are interested, several groups can be formed. Sometimes young people are more comfortable working with their friends, and a group may volunteer expecting to work together. At other times, librarians may need to form groups themselves. Ideally, groups will have a mix of sexes and races, but this might not always be possible. And there are times when a homogeneous group can wield a special power of its own. For instance, Sharon Creech once put together an impressive Readers Theatre composed of female Newbery Award winners, called the Newbery-ettes. When organizing groups, I like to keep in mind that because good literature can transport us beyond who we are, it can be great fun for participants to read parts outside their own gender, ethnicity, age group, time period, or even species.

In any case, it is essential to stress from the beginning that creating a Readers Theatre must be a collaborative effort involving everyone in all phases. Groups should strive to be congenial and do all they can to make the process enjoyable for everyone. Because it is imperative that each person participate in all preparation sessions, practices, and performances, it may be a good idea to consider individual schedules when forming Readers Theatre groups.

Selecting the Text

Once the group has been formed, the next step is selecting the text or texts. This phase involves extensive reading related to the purpose of the performance. I highly recommend that this extensive reading begin with the person organizing the group, so that he or she can appropriately guide participants at this vital stage. When working with author groups, I read everything an author has written before I invite him or her to participate. This prereading not only helps me decide whom I want to invite, but it also prepares me to assist them in their book selections. I ask each author to choose a title from his or her body of work for us to use in our Readers Theatre performance. Sometimes an author knows exactly which book to choose. Often it is his or her most recently published book or one the sponsoring publisher requests. But almost as often, the author turns to me for a suggestion. When this happens, I suggest several titles with reasons. If need be, I point out specific passages I think would work well. But the choice is always the author's.

This same broad-to-narrow guidance can be used for deciding on a purpose or overarching theme for a Readers Theatre presentation as well as specific books to be included. The breadth and number of suggestions depends on the age of the group. The aim is to guide and support, not overwhelm, keeping in mind that the more independence the group has, the more they will gain from the experience and the more they will enjoy the process.

After determining the purpose of the performance and the number of works to be performed, all members of the group read widely to find potential texts that fit the focus. In addition to its content, participants should seriously consider the book's literary format. Picture books, easy readers, novels, poetry collections, short story collections, and informational books often adapt smoothly into Readers Theatre. The graphic novel, however, is one literary format that has proven particularly challenging. Here's a case in point.

Shannon Hale really wanted her graphic novel *Rapunzel's Revenge* to be part of our 2008 ALA Readers Theatre in Anaheim, California. Her first attempt at converting it to a script, which involved a combination of narration, captions, descriptions of images, and speech bubbles, was confusing as a Readers Theatre piece. She revised it to encompass captions expanded to explain some of the image action and dialogue (or exclamatory remarks). Her additions helped the audience grasp the ironic discrepancies between the images and the text.

Hale probably spent more time on her script than any of the other authors I have worked with over the years. The outcome of her diligence was a script the group had lots of fun performing, but the success of the endeavor is clearly related to the author's involvement in the creation of the script. Therefore, popular as graphic novels may be, I would strongly urge that novice Readers Theatre participants shy away from this particular literary format and select books that can be more readily adapted.

Along with content and format, Readers Theatre participants should carefully consider the literary quality of the texts to be used in a performance. Well-written literature uses language that flows naturally and smoothly. Its characters are well drawn and worthy of our attention. It expresses ideas in ways that make readers ponder possibilities rather than dictating decisions to them. It enriches the reader's life experience. Not every book meets these standards, but where better for this literary treasure hunt to take place than a library? And who better to guide the quest than a librarian or a librarian in partnership with a teacher?

As they read, participants recommend texts they might like to use. Everyone reads each recommended book, and the group discusses its merits in terms of the envisioned Readers Theatre performance. Younger groups, such as the second graders in chapter 1's opening scenario, might look for one or two books for their Readers Theatre performance. Upper-elementary and older groups can handle one book for each group member.

> When you [Elizabeth] invited me into the Readers Theatre program for ALA, I was delighted, but I knew (1) I could not adapt any part of a book of mine for this form, and (2) I would need a theatre director to—well, to direct me for performance. You said "Nope, you have to do the adapting and you have to direct the others in performance of your material." I was utterly sure I could not do it. You sent me the scene that Katherine Paterson had taken from her novel, *The Same Stuff as Stars,* and I saw that such an adaptation is perfectly doable. I would simply have to have my brain about me.
>
> As I began the project, the adaptation became less daunting than I'd expected at first. Then it became more daunting. ("Too many threads all tangled up! Oh, woe

When the books have been decided upon, members scrutinize them for passages appropriate for a fifteen- to twenty-minute performance. Picture books generally work well because they tell a complete story. Self-contained sections in novels also work well because they have their own little plots with clearly defined ending points. In addition, look for excerpts with strong emotional content: passages that make readers laugh or cry or fear or wonder. Thought-provoking themes can also be highly appealing. Interesting characters and lively dialogue almost always ensure strong Readers Theatre scripts.

The chapter that Katherine Paterson selected from her novel *The Same Stuff as Stars* is an excellent example of a well-chosen passage. In chapter 11, "Miss Liza at the Library," Angel and her brother, Bernie, go to the library to get a cookbook so eleven-year-old Angel can learn to make gravy. There they encounter Miss Liza, the elderly librarian, who gives Angel a cookbook, along with a book about stars, and Bernie a book about the Stupids. Around this straightforward plot, Paterson weaves an abundance of humor. The children's cantankerous grandma; the belligerent but loving four-year-old Bernie; the kind, deformed librarian; and the slightly confused, but thoughtful, Angel are all intriguing characters. The fast-paced dialogue is both hilarious and touching. And Angel's inner monologue provides much food for thought about human relationships. The chapter stands on its own as a Reading Theatre piece, but it also includes enough hints and references to inspire interest in the larger story.

Discussing works of quality literature, such as Paterson's *The Same Stuff as Stars,* and searching for the exact excerpt to use for a performance can be one of the most enjoyable and rewarding parts of the Readers Theatre experience. Although their age will determine the extent to which they do

---

is me!") As I muddled my way through, I found that I was actually doing it. Just one more example of how it's a good thing when the reach exceeds our grasp. I actually ended up enjoying the task. As it turned out, my colleagues, Tim Wynne-Jones, Cornelia Funke, and David Almond, did just what you said we would do: we directed one another. Each of us cooperated willingly and earnestly. Our performances were homespun, and live. We got to try on voices and miss moments we hoped to get precisely, and the variety of our stories and voices was, I'm guessing, engaging for our ALA audience.

I think it's been demonstrated that kids remember far better what they've performed than what they've merely read or heard. Readers Theatre is perfect for that.
—*Virginia Euwer Wolff*

this, participants of all ages have the opportunity to expand their exposure to good literature through this part of the process.

See chapter 8 for a bibliography of one hundred titles that would make good Readers Theatre.

Divvying Up Tasks

To avoid confusion and ensure that all members have equal amounts of work, the next step is to divide responsibilities among group members. The tasks involved include script development, script notebook organization, directing, stage management, and communication organization. When working with author groups, I ask each author to transform his or her work into a script and serve as director for that piece. Because my goal is to present a model Readers Theatre for educational purposes at professional conferences, I assume the general organizational tasks of script notebook organization, stage management, and communication coordination. Most of these tasks are self-explanatory, but script notebook organizing means making copies of each new version of each script and placing them in a three-ring notebook with subject dividers so readers can access them easily during the presentation.

Librarians and teachers will want to assign responsibilities based on the age, capabilities, and number of group members. Although it may be necessary for adults to assist younger participants, the more appropriate responsibility children and teens assume, the more meaningful their Readers Theatre experience will be. That said, the supervising librarian or teacher must always be aware of what is going on and be ready to gently step in if guidance, support, or problem solving is needed.

When the group consists of the same number of members as there are pieces being performed, each member can assume responsibility for creating, copying, and directing one Readers Theatre piece, and members can work together on stage management and communication organization. As we saw with the five second graders performing in chapter 1, when only one piece is performed, the responsibilities can be divided equally among the readers of that piece. If there is more than one piece but fewer pieces being performed than there are group members, the tasks can be rearranged for each piece. Again, it is important to stress collaboration, cooperation, and congeniality when carrying out group responsibilities.

Transforming the Text into a Script

Using well-written, high-quality literature makes creating a Readers Theatre script a fairly straightforward endeavor. When working with authors,
I tell them that they did most of the work when they wrote the book. Now
all they have to do is divide it into four reading parts. I e-mail a handout,
revised for the most recent professional conference session I have organized, which includes guidelines for creating Readers Theatre experiences,
a portion of a script juxtaposed to its original text, and my commentary
on what the author did to transform the text into the script. Specific directions on the handout for developing scripts include the following points:

- Consider what it would take to change a book into a play as
  you transform the text into a script.
- Eliminate phrases or passages when necessary for a more
  dramatic effect.
- Avoid adding extensive narration or background information.

For some authors, this information is sufficient, and they produce scripts
that need only minor adjustments from me. This was the case with Linda
Sue Park and David Almond. Others go through a series of false starts before the concept clicks into place. Eric Rohmann, Tim Wynne-Jones, and
Lene Kaaberbøl were in this category. I mention this not to belittle these
writers, but because it is instructive.

For one reason or another, each of these authors wrote his or her script
as an entire play. Rohmann added physical descriptions of the kittens and
lots of hilarious dialogue. Wynne-Jones and Kaaberbøl added extensive
stage directions and exposition. I told them they were working way too
hard and putting the emphasis on *theatre* rather than *readers.* I emphasized
sticking to their original words as much as possible and avoiding adding
extensive narration or background material. Sometimes it is necessary to
add a bit of context to a passage, such as a character's name or, in the
case of *A Kitten Tale,* a brief description of the action taking place in an
illustration. It is fine to eliminate phrases or passages when necessary for
a dramatic effect. Generally, speaker signifiers such as "he said" and "she
said" can be deleted. What's important is that the integrity of the work be
maintained even if it is altered slightly.

The result of our correspondences was that Rohmann gradually elimi-nated everything but his original, beautifully crafted words. Wynne-Jones chose a different scene, and Kaaberbøl chose a different book. In the end, all of the authors' scripts were excellent. When we discussed the process of script development in the question-and-answer portion of our conference sessions, Rohmann said it was hard for him as an illustrator to imagine that his sparse words were enough; he feared his peers would think him a slacker if he did not lengthen his contribution. Wynne-Jones said he was so used to the theatre that he just naturally used a conventional dramatic format. Kaaberbøl said the same, telling the audience she laughed when "Elizabeth gently mentioned that now would be a good time to review the guidelines she originally sent." The point of all this is that individuals have their own learning processes; some folks reach the goal directly while oth-ers take a more circuitous route.

The general script development advice for authors applies to children and teens as well. When it comes to physically dividing up the text, it is important to make sure each reader has an equal number of reading oppor-tunities. Assign each reader a letter: A, B, C, D. When a reader plays more than one role, the name of the character or role can be added in parenthe-sis for clarification. It is also possible for several readers to share a lengthy narrator's part, thus becoming Narrator 1, Narrator 2, and so on. To illus-trate, Linda Sue Park's role assignments for *Keeping Score* look like this:

Narrator 1, Radio Announcer, George . . . . Eric Rohmann
Narrator 2 (Maggie's Point of View), Mom . . . . Linda Sue Park
Maggie. . . . . Shannon Hale
Narrator 3, Joey-Mick, Terry . . . . Tobin Andersen

In the author groups, I generally work one-on-one with each author as the script is developed. Then we share them via e-mail so everyone has an opportunity to make suggestions. The authors do not generally have time to make comments at this point. For groups of children and teens, however, this sharing of drafts is an important part of the collaborative process. Even though one member may take the lead when developing the script, all mem-bers need to help by serving as sounding boards, editors, or proofreaders.

See chapter 6 for examples and analysis of portions of Readers Theatre scripts.

Practicing for Successful Performance

In addition to a well-prepared script derived from quality literature, adequate practice is essential for a successful Readers Theatre performance. The author groups spend at least twelve hours together before a performance (eight actually practicing and four sharing meals). They have to do it all in a short period of time since they do not live near one another. As mentioned in chapter 2, not all of this time is on task, but it is all important in terms of group bonding and dynamics. Children and teens should plan on several practice sessions that last an hour or so. During these sessions, necessary modifications become apparent when scripts are read aloud. Time between sessions gives participants opportunities to digest suggestions and reprint scripts. We usually begin with read-throughs sitting around a table and then move onto rehearsals that approximate the actual performance as nearly as possible. The goal is to make every practice both fun and productive.

Arranging the Performing Area

Where the Readers Theatre is performed can affect how it is performed. Arranging the performance area at professional conferences is complicated when authors perform because they require a format unfamiliar to most conference organizers. Fortunately, it does not need to be so complicated for library or school performances. Strive to keep the performing area as simple as possible. Any sort of stage is nice, but not really necessary. Readers can stand behind podia or sit on stools. They can also sit behind tables or on the floor. Scripts can be placed in three-ring notebooks for ease of handling. Arrange for a slanted stand of some sort to hold each reader's notebook so his or her hands are free for gesturing. Music stands work well for this purpose. Microphones can help formalize the situation; lapel microphones are particularly helpful if there will be a large audience. As always, involving the participants in decisions about the performing arrangements is necessary if the experience is to be truly collaborative and reader centered.

See chapter 7, "Pre-Performance Preparation."

Resources

Hale, Shannon and Dean Hale. *Rapunzel's Revenge*. Illustrated by Nathan Hale. New York: Bloomsbury, 2008.

Park, Linda Sue. *Keeping Score*. New York: Clarion, 2008.

Paterson, Katherine. *The Same Stuff as Stars*. New York: Clarion, 2002.

Rohmann, Eric. *A Kitten Tale*. New York: Knopf, 2008.

Wolff, Virginia Euwer. *This Full House*. New York: The Bowen Press/HarperTeen, 2009.

5

Sharing the Pleasure of the Words

Tips for Readers Theatre Performances

━━━━━━━━━━━━━━━

THE AUDIENCE WAITS PATIENTLY WHILE THE CONFERENCE CREW REAR-
ranges the room for the IBBY Readers Theatre performance at the 2008
World Congress in Copenhagen. Months ago, I had given specific instructions about how the stage should be arranged: four podia on a raised platform, one for each of the four authors, and one on the floor for me as
master of ceremonies; five wireless lavaliere microphones, one for each
of us; and one floor microphone for audience members wishing to make
comments after the performance. Our group had practiced knowing that
each person would have a podium on which to place notebooks and a lavaliere microphone to facilitate turning toward one another as they read.
One of our Danish authors confirmed the room setup with the conference
organizer the day before. I was reassured that all would be as we expected
when it came time for the performance. But it isn't.

At the front of the room is a long table, on a raised platform, with five
chairs and two hand microphones. Our group members look at each other, and Lene Kaaberbøl says, "Well, this won't work. We can't hold the
notebooks and the mics at the same time!" I explain to the folks in charge

that the authors need to stand as they perform, and that they *each* need a podium and a wireless lavaliere microphone. The lavaliere microphones appear, but the five podia remain a puzzle until the organizer realizes I am asking for what the Danish call *rostrums.* Unfortunately, there are not five rostrums available. When asked why we need these, I explain that the authors need someplace to rest their notebooks so their hands are free to turn pages and gesture. Would the tall refreshment tables in the lobby do? I am asked. Yes, we all respond in unison.

Once we are situated, the performance begins, and the audience is quickly enthralled by the magic of the authors' words, the interplay among the authors as they read their parts, and the pure pleasure they take in performing together. A delightful surprise occurs when Peter Sís takes a step back from his high table after each time he reads and steps up to it again when he has lines. There is a natural rhythm to his movement, but it is far removed from anything that occurred during our practice sessions. Later, he tells me that standing in front of the audience at the high tables with the other authors reminded him of when he performed with a rock band. His natural inclination was to step back after doing each of his bits to avoid microphone feedback, even though there wasn't any.

Just as when the second graders read for the preschoolers, the 2008 IBBY performance for children's book enthusiasts from all over the world is a hit. The poignant excerpt from Katherine Paterson's *Bread and Roses, Too* calls for Italian accents that the authors clearly enjoy impersonating. Louis Jensen's piece about a dead dog, *Skeleton on Wheels,* elicits a somber tone from the readers. The atmosphere turns eerie when the authors read from Lene Kaaberbøl's *Shadowgate.* Their reading of excerpts from Peter Sís's *The Wall: Growing Up Behind the Iron Curtain* masterfully captures the contrast between the rigidity of life in Communist Czechoslovakia and the fluid dreams of a young artist. All the confusion about the room setup is forgotten as the readers bring their works to life. The careful preparation of the scripts and the extensive practice of the preceding days form an unshakable foundation of confidence; the resultant performance is impressive. (See appendix A for a copy of the session's program.)

Afterward, the Danish conference organizer apologizes for the confusion. He tells me that after seeing what we did, he understands why I insisted, gently but firmly, on the room being organized in such a particular way. We laugh about the rostrum/podium misunderstanding, and

I reassure him the confusion is not cultural. It seems there is frequently some sort of difficulty involved with getting the room set up for a Readers Theatre conference presentation. A few months earlier, at the 2008 ALA Annual Conference in Anaheim, a similar situation occurred. As the audience entered, the hotel conference crew was still rearranging the room according to the instructions I had submitted earlier. Shannon Hale, one of our author-readers, was concerned that we would lose audience members if they had to wait beyond the appointed starting time. So after I told the audience that we required a special setup for our session and the crew was still working on it, Shannon spontaneously started a preperformance audience warm-up. She cracked jokes, teased the other authors, and generally got everyone in good spirits. Again, the delayed start, due to technical difficulties, did not affect the quality of the production once the performance was under way.

> " Readers Theatre was a magic experience. It makes you enjoy and comprehend the book with all the senses. It makes one understand one's own work differently. Most of all it is almost an ancient—round the fire with the stars up in the sky experience in our virtual world. It's a great educational experience. Vivid memory: I will never forget the Danish writer, Louis Jensen, and the dead dog! —*Peter Sís*

I mention these technical difficulties not to make librarians and teachers apprehensive about Readers Theatre performances, but rather as cautionary tales to consider when preparing for a performance. I offer the following tips for helping Readers Theatre performances run as smoothly as possible.

KISS, or Keep it Super-Simple

The more elaborate the performance strives to be, the more potential there is for something to go amiss. For me, the most effective way to prevent a performance from getting unduly complicated is to keep the emphasis on *readers* not *theatre*. As I mentioned before, this means focusing on the author's words and how they are read. In this high-tech age, we are tempted to use technology just because we can. That said, it's important to determine whether technical enhancements are essential to conveying the author's words, possibly necessary but cumbersome, or just theatrically entertaining.

The microphone question is a case in point. Individual microphones were essential for the professional conference performances described at the beginning of this chapter. When audiences number from three hundred to seven hundred people, the author's words cannot be heard by all without amplification. Past performances demonstrate the importance of readers turning toward one another in dialogue exchanges and changing podium positions between each piece. Handheld microphones are out of the question because readers need to turn pages in the script notebooks and gesture at opportune times. Podium microphones don't pick up readers' voices if they turn their heads to talk directly to one another. Lapel microphones that are wired to the podium get tangled when readers change positions between pieces. Wireless lavaliere microphones may be expensive to rent and a bit tricky to operate, but they are essential for this situation. However, when children perform for family, friends, and other students, microphones, although they do formalize the situation in a way that may appeal to children and teens, may not be necessary at all. As can be seen from the opening examples, not using microphones would certainly simplify the performance situation.

I am in the habit of projecting a cover image of each book, using either an overhead projector or an LCD projector, while the excerpt from that book is being read. This is tantamount to holding up the book while booktalking it; it helps potential readers find it more easily in the library or bookstore. Although a projected image adds a useful touch with a large audience, it can be a bit cumbersome, and is not essential to a successful performance. There are certainly simpler ways to display the book's cover for smaller audiences. The children in the opening scenario in chapter 1 each read from the actual book, holding the book in such a way that the cover could be seen by children seated on the floor. Enlarged covers could be displayed on easels or the books propped up on a nearby table. Again, the simplest method will often be the best for the situation.

Speaking of visuals, in question-and-answer sessions following professional conference presentations in which we have read from a picture book, someone inevitably asks about projecting the illustrations to accompany the text being read. My answer is there is nothing wrong with doing this, and certainly the illustrations and text were designed to go together, but because Readers Theatre performances focus on the author's words, the projected images may actually detract from the verbal images being painted by the words. A glitch with the technology projecting the images would certainly detract from the reading. Again, keeping it simple by not including illustrations seems the best approach. As discussed in earlier chapters, this involves selecting books with words that can stand alone with only an occasional phrase or line added to provide vital information supplied by an illustration.

Adding music is another topic to consider. When we were working on the scripts for the 2007 ALA Readers Theatre in Washington, D.C., Virginia Euwer Wolff wanted to include a short piece of recorded music when the group read from *The Mozart Season*. I didn't want to disappoint her, so I told her I would find a way to include it. The program person and I arranged for the convention techies to insert a patch into the audio system so I could push a button and play the music on cue. We had it worked out during our practice sessions, but when the readers were performing, there was a long pause while they waited for the background music to begin before continuing their lines. The pause was so awkward that the readers instinctively went ahead, and we never did have the musical background the author had envisioned with her piece. I thought about it a lot afterwards and concluded that it would have been better to just say no in the first place rather than get too complicated. It's best to keep it super-simple.

Interestingly enough, the 2007 ALA group came to this same conclusion regarding music and Tim Wynne-Jones's *Rex Zero and the End of the World*. The passage he selected ended with a reference to the land beyond the neighborhood being "the twilight zone." Since we were already planning music for *The Mozart Season,* I thought it would be fun to play a few notes of *The Twilight Zone* theme at the end of *Rex Zero*. I found the music on the Internet, but when we were practicing, it was so hard to get the timing right that we agreed the group should just vocalize the *do-do-do-do, do-do-do-do*'s themselves. It was an effective, audience-pleasing ending. Why use complicated technology when simple voices will do?

Wynne-Jones brought up the question of props when he was preparing his script for *The Boy in the Burning House*. Because one reader would be covering more than one part, he wondered if that person could wear a collar when reading the priest's part and glasses when reading the librarian's part. I laughed when I read his suggestion. It brought to mind an image of girls at camp after dinner putting their napkins above their lips like moustaches and lowering their voices to say, "You must pay the rent," then making their napkins into hair bows and raising their voices to say, "I can't pay the rent" then making their napkins into bow ties and saying in a regular voice, "I'll pay the rent," followed by "My hero" with napkin/hair bow and "Curses, foiled again" with napkin/moustache.

With that humorous image in mind, I explained that props would be unnecessary because the readers could distinguish the various parts with voice changes. I also pointed out that with all we would be doing during the performance, juggling props could be complicated and might actually detract from the author's words. At practice, when the author saw how much we were dealing with, he, too, laughed at the idea of trying to incorporate props into the performance.

Questions about props and costumes often come up at professional conferences. I always respond that because Readers Theatre is minimalist theatre, props and costumes are unnecessary. A teacher once asked what it would hurt if the children wore bunny ears and hopped around when reading something like Candace Fleming's *Muncha! Muncha! Muncha!* My answer was that it didn't hurt anything; it just wasn't Readers Theatre. The more things the children and adults have to keep track of—script notebooks, bunny ears, movements, etc.—the further the focus is removed from the author's words and their power in and of themselves to evoke strong reactions from the audience. Along this line, I stress that readers wear plain black clothing to keep things simple and focused. Even jewelry or colored headbands can detract from the reading of the words. Words and voices really are enough for this particular art form.

Be Prepared

Carefully crafted scripts and extensive rehearsal sessions are essential for successful performances. Preparation includes practice reading the scripts not only fluently, but dramatically as well. Readers can show emotion by

A story can come alive in many ways: whispered at night by a child who reads it secretly under the cover of a warm bed; read by parents, teachers, actors in living rooms and on theatre stages. Nothing wakes printed words better from their slumber on the page than the human voice. But there is one especially magical way to do this. I rarely saw my story come to life as vividly as when I had the pleasure to be invited by Elizabeth Poe to a Readers Theatre. I traveled to Washington, D. C., not really knowing what to expect. But suddenly there I was, in a room with three other writers and we summoned each others' char-

altering pace and volume. They can use different voices for different characters. They can give the audience visual cues through facial expressions and hand gestures. Although stage notes are not part of the scripts, readers often jot notes to themselves regarding particular vocal adjustments and bodily maneuvers. Such performance suggestions made during rehearsals by other group members enhance the reading without detracting from the actual words. For example, when the 2007 ALA Readers Theatre was practicing Cornelia Funke's *The Thief Lord,* the group decided that David Almond, who was reading the part of Ricco, should look scared and make his voice pleading when he says, "Please! Please don't shoot." Then as Virginia Euwer Wolff, taking the part of the narrator, reads, "Ricco held up his hands," David/Ricco should hold up his hands. Nothing too elaborate or distracting here, just natural vocal and bodily expressions elicited by the script.

Readers should be familiar enough with their scripts that they can look up whenever possible. Maintaining eye contact with the audience or using off-stage focus is a good idea. It is most effective if readers who are speaking to each other turn toward one another. To facilitate these exchanges, readers who will be speaking primarily to each other need to stand or sit next to each other. When doing multiple pieces, the readers sharing dialogues will change from piece to piece, making it necessary for readers to rearrange themselves between pieces. Determining each reader's podium position in the various pieces takes a bit of orchestrating. When we were working on position changes for the 2008 IBBY, Peter Sís even drew a diagram to help the group prepare for moves between readings.

Along with readers preparing their voices and movements, there are several physical aspects that also require proper preparation. The first is the script notebooks. These three-ring notebooks contain the scripts for the various pieces that will be performed. Each piece should be placed

acters by lending them our voices. What a perfect way to enter each other's imagined worlds. And how in my boldest writer dreams would I have ever have imagined David Almond, one of my most admired writers, would become my Sad Knight from *Igraine, the Brave* and read a dialogue with me as Igraine? The knight will forever have his accent now. I cannot imagine any better way to introduce children and grownups to the magic of story telling than a readers theatre. And it doesn't need much, not even a stage! Just a few passionate readers in a room who lend their voices to their favorite character. Try it! I am sure you will get addicted to the experience. —*Cornelia Funke*

behind a subject divider for easy access. The pages need to turn easily. The notebooks should be no thicker than necessary—a half inch is usually fine. Black notebooks are the most unobtrusive, particularly if the readers are dressed in black. It is wise to have two extra copies of these notebooks. I had one author who forgot to bring hers to the performance and another who lost hers after the first rehearsal. Fortunately, I had extras.

The second helpful physical aspect is the creation of a program for the audience. This can be as simple as a list of the books from which performers will be reading or as complex as a playbill that provides information about each of the cast members. Because my purpose is to educate, I also include a handout along with the program on how to create a Readers Theatre experience in one's own library or classroom. (See appendix A for program from 2008 IBBY Readers Theatre.)

The third physical necessity is the room arrangement. As shown in the scenarios at the opening of this chapter, the room setup is crucial. Determine what your group needs as early as possible and share your plan with the person who is responsible for getting furniture and equipment. You might draw a diagram of how the room should look, where the readers will sit or stand, where they will place their notebooks, and where the audience will sit. It is a good idea to double-check the physical arrangements before the actual performance time. If electronic equipment is required, make sure it works properly. I have learned that it never hurts to be over-conscientious in an effort to ensure that all is prepared for the performance.

Know Your Bottom Lines

Even when one is well prepared, questions will arise throughout the process of creating a Readers Theatre experience. Keeping your purpose and vision in mind can help you make decisions that keep the project on course. The room arrangement situations described earlier are a case in point. I knew from experience that the group needed a specific setup for a successful presentation. It was important for me to assert, gently but firmly, that we could not begin until certain arrangements were in place. There have also been times when I have had to tell publishers that unless an author can make our practice schedule, he or she will not be able to participate. I mention this issue because when we work with children and teens, we are often asked to make decisions requiring knowledge of our philosophical bottom line. The more groups I organize, the more confident I am in my experience and judgment. Being able to explain those judgments generally makes them acceptable.

In addition to a philosophical bottom line, there are also financial and legal bottom lines to consider. Generally speaking, using reader-created scripts is less expensive than buying books containing prefabricated scripts because the literary works are already part of the library's collection. However, extra copies may need to be purchased, not just for the readers, but to meet the demand for the book the performance will create. Supplies, such as three-ring notebooks, subject dividers, highlighting pens, and paper may also be needed. Even though it need not be large, a budget can provide necessary financial parameters for participants and administrators.

Copyright laws provide a legal bottom line for Readers Theatre productions. It is considered fair use to use an excerpt from a book for the type of educational purposes that would take place in a school or library setting, as long as admission is not charged. When the question of copyright arose in a panel discussions following one of our ALA Readers Theatre presentations, I asked the publishers in the audience to respond. They said there was no legal problem with using the book once for educational purposes, but librarians may want to check with the particular publisher to be on the safe, as well as courteous, side.

Go with the Flow

Sometimes the situation is such that all one can do is go with the flow. This is how I have come to view difficulties with room arrangements at professional conferences. What we are asking for is so unusual that it rarely occurs without timely intervention on my part. Taking a cue from the improvised explanation I gave to the audience in Copenhagen while the technicians were arranging the podia and equipment, I now make setting up the room part of the program. I divide the Readers Theatre program into acts and call act 1 Setting the Stage. After using this approach at the 2010 ALA Readers Theatre in Washington, D.C., and the 2010 IBBY Readers Theatre in Santiago de Compostela, Spain, I plan to keep it as part of the presentation. After all, the purpose of the presentation is to help librarians and teachers learn how to create a Readers Theatre experience in their own libraries, and this is a natural way to provide essential information.

Should the room happen to be all set to go when we arrive, I will point out the particulars of our arrangements before we begin the performance. In either case, I intend to go with the flow.

I learned a lot about going with the flow from Katherine Paterson when I helped her organize the academic portion of a Readers Theatre presentation at the 2004 IBBY World Congress in Capetown. When one of the American authors she invited cancelled at the last minute, she quickly agreed to have a South African actor to take his place, even though he was not a children's author. When, the night before the performance, one of the South African authors hesitatingly expressed discomfort at having her signature poem read by four people, Paterson graciously told her she could read it as a solo piece. Her bottom line was making people feel comfortable. A tremendously successful Readers Theatre performance was the result.

Sometimes going with the flow means the organizer, or the librarian-teacher in charge, needs to step in and perform a task herself. Two cases in point occurred when it was not possible for authors to convert their books into scripts themselves. In the spring of 2007, Cornelia Funke was deeply involved in the filming of the *Inkheart* movie. We decided to collaborate in reverse, with me developing the scripts for *Igraine the Brave* and *The Thief Lord* and her approving them and directing the group in their reading. In the summer of 2008 Peter Sís had heavy travel commitments prior to the IBBY World Congress in Copenhagen. Not having time to convert *The Wall* into a script himself, he readily accepted my offer to take on the task. The format of the book made this a complex conversion, and I enjoyed the challenge. In this case, he had not seen the script prior to rehearsal, so I served as its director as well.

Although I took deep pleasure in the way these three pieces turned out, and I believe it was necessary for me to step in for the good of the presentation as a whole, I must caution myself about becoming *too* involved and regularly taking on responsibilities that should be collaborative. As adults working with children and teens we often find it easier or more straightforward to perform tasks like writing the scripts ourselves, but this runs counter to the philosophy in which I so firmly believe. Going with the flow is sometimes necessary, but my bottom line is to allow participants to be involved as much as possible with the process as well as the presentation. Quite simply, the more readers are involved, the more fun they have.

Have fun! Yes, fun is first and foremost. Readers should genuinely enjoy themselves when giving Readers Theatre performances. Chances are that if children and teens have enjoyed the process—the extensive reading to select the appropriate text, the deep involvement with the author's words that comes with creating a script, the intensive practicing with peers, and the relationships formed with helping adults—they will also enjoy the performance. And chances are that that enjoyment will lead to further enjoyment of quality literature, a pleasure that can last a lifetime.

Resources

Fleming, Candace. *Muncha! Muncha! Muncha!* Illustrated by G. Brian Karas. New York: Atheneum, 2002.

Funke, Cornelia. *The Thief Lord.* New York: Chicken House, 2002.

———. *Igraine the Brave.* New York: Chicken House, 2007.

Jensen, Louis. *Skeleton on Wheels.* Published in Danish as *Skelettet på hjul.* Denmark: Gyldendal, 1999.

Kaaberbøl, Lene. *Shadowgate.* Published in Danish as *Skyggeporten.* Copenhagen: Forlaget Forum, 2006.

Paterson, Katherine. *Bread and Roses, Too.* New York: Clarion, 2006.

Sís, Peter. *The Wall: Growing Up Behind the Iron Curtain.* New York: Frances Foster/Farrar Straus Giroux, 2007.

Wolff, Virginia Euwer. *The Mozart Season.* New York: Scholastic, 1991.

Wynne-Jones, Tim. *The Boy in the Burning House.* New York: Melanie Kroupa/Farrar Straus Giroux, 2000.

———. *Rex Zero and the End of the World.* New York: Melanie Kroupa/Farrar Straus Giroux, 2007.

Part II

A How-To Guide

6

Adapting Literature to Script

Examples and Analysis of Portions of Readers Theatre Scripts

DURING THE QUESTION-AND-ANSWER SESSION FOLLOWING A READERS Theatre presentation at an International Reading Association conference, an audience member suggested that I include an example of a Readers Theatre script in my handout. Taking this excellent suggestion to heart, my handout now provides an example based on one of the pieces read in that session's performance. It includes a portion of the original text, its corresponding script, and commentary explaining decisions made to convert the text to script. I follow this same format here, giving multiple examples for various types of books. The examples within each type generally progress from the simpler books to adapt to the more complex.

Some of these examples are excerpts from scripts read at professional conferences. When working with authors to develop these scripts, I began by providing some general instructions along with a copy of a script Katherine Paterson created and a copy of the chapter in *The Same Stuff as Stars* from which it was developed. She generously allowed me to do this; the other authors found her work a helpful model.

Other examples are my own, created to demonstrate how books with certain characteristics can be used for Readers Theatre. In developing these examples, I am reminded once again that selecting the right book and the right passage is key to creating a viable script. I am also reminded how rewarding it is to convert texts to scripts and how important it is encourage young patrons to do this themselves.

Readers are designated by letters such as A, B, C, D. The roles they read are indicated above the script and abbreviated after the letter within the script for clarification. I use this format rather than readers' actual names because it is easier to make modifications when necessary, including substituting a new person for a reader in case of emergency. *Position* refers to the order in which the readers stand on the stage. For example: D, A, C, B would mean that D stands on the far left and B stands on the far right, with the others between them.

Picture Books

Because Readers Theatre primarily involves words, it may come as a surprise that picture books are excellent sources for scripts. Because of their length and focus, however, picture books are excellent candidates. The ones that work best are those that tell a complete story through narration and dialogue. Of course pictures enhance the story, even add a new layer or dimension to it, but the story generally makes a certain sense without the illustrations. An occasional narrative reliance on illustration is not a problem, as can be seen in the example from Eric Rohmann's *A Kitten Tale*.

Wild About Books **by Judy Sierra**

Text from pages 1–6 of unpaged book:

It started the summer of 2002,
When the Springfield librarian, Molly McGrew,
By mistake drove her bookmobile into the zoo.

Molly opened the door, and she let down the stair,
Turned on the computer, and sat in her chair.

At first all the animals watched from a distance,
But Molly could conquer the strongest resistance.

By reading aloud from the good Dr. Seuss,
She quickly attracted a mink and a moose,

A wombat, an oryx, a lemur, a lynx.
Eight elephant calves, and a family of skinks.

In a flash every beast in the zoo was stampeding
To learn all about this new something called *reading.*

Text converted to Readers Theatre script:

A: Narrator 1
B: Narrator 2
C: Narrator 3
Positions: A B C

A (Nar 1):   It started the summer of 2002,
When the Springfield librarian, Molly McGrew,
By mistake drove her bookmobile into the zoo.

B (Nar 2):   Molly opened the door, and she let down the stair,
Turned on the computer, and sat in her chair.

C (Nar 3):   At first all the animals watched from a distance,
But Molly could conquer the strongest resistance.

A (Nar 1):   By reading aloud from the good Dr. Seuss,
She quickly attracted a mink and a moose,

B (Nar 2):   A wombat, an oryx, a lemur, a lynx.
Eight elephant calves, and a family of skinks.

C (Nar 3):   In a flash every beast in the zoo was stampeding
To learn all about this new something called reading.

Commentary

Sierra's text took very little to convert it to a script. All I did was assign parts according to the rhyming lines. Although Marc Brown's vivid illustrations exuberantly portray the characters and their actions, the lines themselves actually tell the whole story. Nothing needs to be added, subtracted, or modified. I designed the script for three readers, but it would also work fine with four or five readers.

Bubble Trouble by Margaret Mahy

Text from pages 6–10:

Little Mabel blew a bubble, and it caused a lot of trouble . . .
Such a lot of bubble trouble in a bibble-bobble way.
First it broke away from Mabel as it bobbed across the table,
where it bobbled over Baby, and it wafted him away.

The baby didn't quibble. He began to smile and dibble,
for he liked the wibble-wobble of the bubble in the air.
But Mabel ran for cover as the bubble bobbed above her,
and she shouted out for Mother, who was putting up her hair.

At the sudden cry of trouble, Mother took off at the double,
for the squealing left her reeling, made her terrified and tense,
saw the bubble for a minute, with the baby bobbing in it,
as it bibbled by the letterbox and bobbed across the fence.

Text converted to Readers Theatre script:

A: Narrator 1
B: Narrator 2
C: Narrator 3
D: Narrator 4
Positions: A B C D

A (Nar 1): Little Mabel blew a bubble, and it caused a lot of trouble . . .

B (Nar 2): Such a lot of bubble trouble in a bibble-bobble way.

C (Nar 3): First it broke away from Mabel as it bobbed across the table,

D (Nar 4): where it bobbled over Baby, and it wafted him away.

A (Nar 1): The baby didn't quibble. He began to smile and dibble,

B (Nar 2): for he liked the wibble-wobble of the bubble in the air.

C (Nar 3): But Mabel ran for cover as the bubble bobbed above her,

D (Nar 4): and she shouted out for Mother, who was putting up her hair.

A (Nar 1): At the sudden cry of trouble, Mother took off at the double,

B (Nar 2): for the squealing left her reeling, made her terrified and tense,

C (Nar 3): saw the bubble for a minute, with the baby bobbing in it,

D (Nar 4): as it bibbled by the letterbox and bobbed across the fence.

Commentary

As in the case with *Wild About Books,* I did not have to alter the text one bit when converting it to a Readers Theatre script. The text, a series of quatrains, lends itself perfectly to four readers, with each reading one line of each verse. While quite appropriate for young listeners, the complexity of this delightful linguistic romp makes it excellent fare for older Readers Theatre participants to read to an audience of all ages. In this case, it seems desirable for the readers to read in the order in which they are standing (A, B, C, D), accentuating the rhythm and flow of Mahy's words. Whether read in excerpts or in its entirety, the effervescent story will send the audience bobbling to Polly Dunbar's lively illustrations for even more bubble trouble fun.

Mike Mulligan and His Steam Shovel by Virginia Lee Burton

Text from pages 20–22:

When they got there they found that the selectmen were just decid-ing who should dig the cellar for the new town hall. Mike Mulligan spoke to Henry B. Swap, one of the selectmen.

"I heard," he said, "that you are going to build a new town hall. Mary Anne and I will dig the cellar for you in just one day."

"What!" said Henry B. Swap. "Dig a cellar in a day! It would take a hundred men at least a week to dig the cellar for our new town hall."

"Sure," said Mike, "but Mary Anne can dig as much in a day as a hundred men can dig in a week."

Though he had never been quite sure that this was true.

Then he added,

"If we can't do it, you won't have to pay."

Henry B. Swap thought that this would be an easy way to get part of the cellar dug for nothing, so he smiled in rather a mean way and gave the job of digging the cellar of the new town hall to Mike Mulligan and Mary Anne.

They started in early the next morning just as the sun was coming up. Soon a little boy came along.

"Do you think you will finish by sundown?" he said to Mike Mulligan.

"Sure," said Mike, "if you stay and watch us. We always work faster and better when someone is watching us."

So the little boy stayed to watch.

Text converted to Readers Theatre script:

A: Narrator
B: Mike Mulligan
C: Henry B. Swap
D: Little Boy
Positions: A C B D

A (Nar): When they got there they found that the selectmen were just deciding who should dig the cellar for the new town hall. Mike Mulligan spoke to Henry B. Swap, one of the selectmen.

B (Mike):   *(Turning toward Henry B. Swap)* I heard that you are going to build a new town hall. Mary Anne and I will dig the cellar for you in just one day.

C (Henry):   *(Turning toward Mike Mulligan)* What! Dig a cellar in a day! It would take a hundred men at least a week to dig the cellar for our new town hall.

B (Mike):   Sure, but Mary Anne can dig as much in a day as a hundred men can dig in a week.

A (Nar):   Though he had never been quite sure that this was true. Then he added,

B (Mike):   If we can't do it, you won't have to pay.

A (Nar):   Henry B. Swap thought that this would be an easy way to get part of the cellar dug for nothing, so he smiled in rather a mean way and gave the job of digging the cellar of the new town hall to Mike Mulligan and Mary Anne. They started in early the next morning just as the sun was coming up. Soon a little boy came along.

D (Boy):   *(Turning toward Mike Mulligan)* Do you think you will finish by sundown?

B (Mike):   *(Turning toward Little Boy)* Sure, if you stay and watch us. We always work faster and better when someone is watching us.

A (Nar):   So the little boy stayed to watch.

Commentary

This text converted easily into a script. All I had to do was delete the speaker signifiers, position the readers so they could turn and talk to one another, and add cues to let them know when to do this. Because there are more than four parts in the entire book, readers will need to double up on parts and change their voices to fit the character. Designating two more narrators would probably be a good idea, particularly in the beginning.

We used this passage to conclude the 2010 ALA Readers Theatre in Washington, D.C. After A read the last line, the group paused and then read in unison: "And we always read smoother and better when we have an audience. Thanks for staying to listen!"

In addition to being an effective conclusion to the performance, this invented line served as a natural segue to the instructional part of the program, which focused on the benefits and how-tos of Readers Theatre. It demonstrates how text can be manipulated for the purposes of performance.

A Kitten Tale by Eric Rohmann

Text from pages 14–20 of unpaged book:

Then one morning the kittens woke to snow.
But the fourth kitten didn't hide.
He jumped and rolled and laughed.
"Snow! It's cold and wet and covers everything!"
"We'll be right out!"

Text converted to Readers Theatre script:

A: Narrator 2/ First Kitten (Ginger Kitten)
B: Narrator 1/ Second Kitten (Blue Kitten)
C: Narrator 3/ Third Kitten (Brown Spotted Kitten)
D: Narrator 4/ Fourth Kitten (Yellow Kitten)
Positions: A B D C

B (Nar 2):   Then one winter morning the kittens woke to snow.

A (Nar 1):   The first kitten darted under the table.

B (Nar 2):   The second kitten burrowed under the rug.

C (Nar 3):   The third kitten ducked into the closet.

D (Nar 4):   But the fourth kitten didn't hide.

C (Nar 3):   He leaped out into the snow.

B (Nar 1):   He jumped and rolled and laughed.

D (4th K):   Snow! It's cold and wet and covers everything!

(The other three kittens all look at each other and smile.)

A, B, C (1st, 2nd, 3rd Ks): We'll be right out!

D (4th K):   I can't wait!

Commentary

This picture book was a bit more complicated to work with because some of the story is told through the pictures. When working on this script, Eric Rohmann created lines to describe the pictures showing where the three kittens that were afraid of snow hid. He also added a line to let the audience know that the fourth kitten leaped out into the snow, and he directed the three inside kitten readers to look at each other and smile, as the kittens do in the illustration. Having all three kittens read their last line together plays on the humor of the kittens smiling at one another and sets up the fourth kitten for a dramatically effective final line.

As the book's author and illustrator, it was not difficult for Rohmann to translate the pictures into words for the purpose of a Readers Theatre performance. As mentioned in chapter 1, translating from to pictures to words requires children to grasp both the verbal and visual aspects of the story. Writing in the style of the author can be an interesting challenge. Because each word of the text in a picture book with few words adds to the rhythm and integrity of the reading, even speaker signifiers need to remain. (Note that I designed the opening script in chapter 1 for five readers for ease of illustration. Rohmann's script was for four readers, so he had readers taking parts as both narrators and kittens.)

Easy Readers

Easy readers often consist of one or more self-contained stories that can readily translate into Readers Theatre scripts. The beauty of these books is that young readers can read them and thus be involved in Readers Theatre experiences.

Zelda and Ivy: The Runaways by Laura McGee Kvasnosky

Text from pages 1–5:

"Dad's making cucumber sandwiches for lunch," said Ivy.

"Not again!" said Zelda. "That's it. I'm running away."

Zelda stuffed her lucky jewel, PJs, blanket, writer's notebook, and an extra pair of socks into her suitcase.

"I'm coming too," said Ivy.

She packed her Princess Mimi doll, PJs, tea set, and Go Fish cards.

Zelda marched across the backyard. Ivy followed.

Zelda spread her blanket behind the butterfly bush. "Here's a good spot," she said. "We can see the house, but no one in the house can see us."

The Fox sisters peeked through the bush at their parents.

"Mom and Dad will really miss us," said Ivy.

"Yes," said Zelda. "They'll be sorry they made us cucumber sandwiches."

Text converted to Readers Theatre script:

A: Ivy
B: Zelda
C: Narrator 1 (associated with Zelda)
D: Narrator 2 (associated with Ivy)
Positions: D A B C

A (Ivy):   Dad's making cucumber sandwiches for lunch, Zelda.

B (Zelda):   Not again, Ivy! That's it. I'm running away.

C (Nar 1):   Zelda stuffed her lucky jewel, PJs, blanket, writer's notebook, and an extra pair of socks into her suitcase.

A (Ivy):   I'm coming too.

D (Nar 2):   Ivy packed her Princess Mimi doll, PJs, tea set, and Go Fish cards.

C (Nar 1):   Zelda marched across the backyard.

D (Nar 2):   Ivy followed.

C (Nar 1):   Zelda spread her blanket behind the butterfly bush.

B (Zelda):   Here's a good spot. We can see the house, but no one in the house can see us.

C and D (Nars 1, 2): The Fox sisters peeked through the bush at their parents.

A (Ivy):   Mom and Dad will really miss us.

B (Zelda):   Yes. They'll be sorry they made us cucumber sandwiches.

Commentary

This text needed only minor revisions to transform it into a Readers Theatre script. The main thing I did was eliminate expressions such as "Ivy said" and "Zelda said." Then, to clarify who is speaking or acting, I inserted Ivy or Zelda's name into the text. I divided the narrator's part into two, one associated with each character. When referring to the sisters acting together, the narrators speak in unison. Having two readers as narrators quickens the pace, adds variety, and provides parts for four readers rather than three.

Marvin One Too Many by Katherine Paterson

Text from pages 41–48:

"Will you read to me?" he asked.
"Sure," said Dad.
May found a funny poem about a cow for Dad to read.

Dad put his finger under each word.
" 'I never saw a purple cow,
I never hope to see one.
But I can tell you anyhow,
I'd rather see than be one.' "

"OW!" said Marvin.
"Are you hurt?" asked Dad.
"No!" said Marvin. "See? OW!
"Cuh-OW. COW!"

"You are reading!" said Dad.
"You read 'cow'!"
"I love cows," said Marvin.
" 'Cow' is my favorite word.

Did you know my name moos
Just like a cow?" asked Marvin.
"How can Marvin moo?" asked Dad.
"Mmmmmmar-vin!" said Marvin.

"You're right, Marvin!
The M moos, just like a cow."
Just then all the lights came on.
Soon they heard the snowplow.
"Yippee!" said Marvin.

"Tomorrow I can tell Ms. Brr-OW-na
about all Mmmmmar-vin's cuh-OWs!"

"Tell Ms. Brr-OW-na for me
That we will read together every night.

Guys who take a little
Longer need to stick together," said Dad.
And that is h-OW Mmmmmar-vin started reading and
Stopped being Marvin one too many.

Text converted to Readers Theatre script:

A: (Marvin)
B: (Dad)
C: (Narrator)
Positions: B A C

A (Mar):   Will you read to me, Dad?

B (Dad):   Sure, Marvin.

C (Nar):   May found a funny poem about a cow for Dad to read.
              Dad put his finger under each word.

B (Dad):   I never saw a purple cow,
              I never hope to see one.
              But I can tell you anyhow,
              I'd rather see than be one.

A (Mar):   OW!

B (Dad):   Are you hurt?

A (Mar):   No! See? OW!
              Cuh-OW. COW!

B (Dad):   You are reading!
              You read 'cow'!

A (Mar):	I love cows.
	Cow is my favorite word.
	Did you know my name moos
	just like a cow?

| B (Dad): | How can Marvin moo? |

| A (Mar): | Mmmmmmar-vin! |

| B (Dad): | You're right, Marvin. |
| | The M moos, just like a cow. |

A (Mar):	Yippee!
	Tomorrow I can tell Ms. Brr-OW-na about all Mmmm
	mar-vin's cuh-OWs!

B (Dad)	Tell Ms. Brr-OW-na for me that we will read together
	every night.
	Guys who take a little
	longer need to stick together.

| C (Nar): | And that is h-OW Mmmmmar-vin started reading. |

Commentary

Converting Paterson's text to a Readers Theatre script required only slightly more modification than did Kvasnosky's. Here, too, I removed expressions such as "asked Dad" and "said Marvin" and identified the speakers by inserting their names in the initial lines.

In addition, because I wanted to present a self-contained excerpt, I deleted three lines ("Just then all the lights came on"; "Soon they heard the snowplow"; "and stopped being Marvin one too many"). These are the type of modifications children can make when they understand that there are several aspects to the story and that by focusing on only one, they make it easier for the audience to understand the excerpt.

The script divided naturally into three reading parts. If the whole book were to be read, more readers could be added, thus eliminating the need for young readers to double up on parts.

Novels

Novels require at least two levels of selection: the book itself and the portion or portions to actually read. I have included examples from a rather large sampling of novels of various types and reading levels. If the group will be reading from several novels, selecting a chapter from each generally works well. The selection does not have to convey the complete story line, but rather an intriguing part that will inspire audience members to read or reread the novel. (See chapter 3.) If the group is reading from one novel, three or four carefully chosen parts can convey the gist of the entire story. In either case, the selections need to be compelling reading that will give the audience an engaging listening experience.

The Penderwicks: A Summer Tale of Four Sisters, Two Rabbits, and a Very Interesting Boy by Jeanne Birdsall

Text from pages 2–3:

"It's Batty's fault," said Skye.

"It is not," Batty said.

"Of course it is," said Skye. "We wouldn't be lost if Hound hadn't eaten the map, and Hound wouldn't have eaten the map if you hadn't hidden your sandwich in it."

"Maybe it's fate that Hound ate the map. Maybe we'll discover something wonderful while we're lost," said Jane.

"We'll discover that when I'm in the backseat for too long with my younger sisters, I go insane and murder them," said Skye.

"Steady, troops," said Mr. Penderwick. "Rosalind, how about a game?"

"Let's do I Went to the Zoo and I Saw," said Rosalind. "I went to the zoo and I saw an anteater. Jane?"

"I went to the zoo and I saw an anteater and a buffalo," said Jane.

Batty was between Jane and Skye, so it was her turn next. "I went to the zoo and I saw an anteater, a buffalo, and a cangaroo."

"*Kangaroo* starts with a *k*, not a *c*," said Skye.

"It does not. It starts with a *c*, like *cat*," said Batty.

"Just take your turn, Skye," said Rosalind.

"There's no point playing if we don't do it right."

Rosalind, who was sitting in the front with Mr. Penderwick, turned around and gave Skye her oldest-sister glare. It wouldn't do much, Rosalind knew. After all, Skye was only one year younger than she was. But it might quiet her long enough for Rosalind to concentrate on where they were going. They really were badly lost. This trip should have taken an hour and a half, and already they'd been on the road for three.

Text converted to Readers Theatre script:

A: Skye
B: Batty
C: Jane
D: Mr. Penderwick
E: Rosalind
F: Narrator
Positions: D E A B C F

A (Skye): It's Batty's fault.

B (Batty): It is not.

A (Skye): Of course it is. We wouldn't be lost if Hound hadn't eaten the map, and Hound wouldn't have eaten the map if you hadn't hidden your sandwich in it.

C (Jane): Maybe it's fate that Hound ate the map. Maybe we'll discover something wonderful while we're lost.

A (Skye): We'll discover that when I'm in the backseat for too long with my younger sisters, I go insane and murder them.

D (Mr. P.): Steady, troops. Rosalind, how about a game?

E (Rosa): Let's do I Went to the Zoo and I Saw. I went to the zoo and I saw an anteater. Jane?

C (Jane):   I went to the zoo and I saw an anteater and a buffalo.

F (Nar):   Batty was between Jane and Skye, so it was her turn next.

B (Batty):   I went to the zoo and I saw an anteater, a buffalo, and a cangaroo.

A (Skye):   *Kangaroo* starts with a *k,* not a *c.*

B (Batty):   It does not. It starts with a *c,* like *cat.*

E (Rosa):   Just take your turn, Skye.

A (Skye):   There's no point playing if we don't do it right.

F (Nar):   Rosalind, who was sitting in the front with Mr. Penderwick, turned around and gave Skye her oldest-sister glare. It wouldn't do much, Rosalind knew. After all, Skye was only one year younger than she was. But it might quiet her long enough for Rosalind to concentrate on where they were going. They really were badly lost. This trip should have taken an hour and a half, and already they'd been on the road for three.

Commentary

When I was writing a *BookNotes* educators guide for *The Penderwicks: A Summer Tale of Four Sisters, Two Rabbits, and a Very Interesting Boy,* I used this passage and script to demonstrate how children can prepare their own scripts for *The Penderwicks.* I chose this section primarily because the conversion is straightforward. All I had to do was eliminate the speaker signifiers and assign parts. Using six readers makes the script easy to prepare and read because there is no doubling up on parts. I also like this passage because Birdsall uses broad strokes to quickly paint the personalities of the sisters, the family dynamics, and the humor that awaits the reader. It is an effective introduction to a book that is a natural choice when looking for a children's novel to perform as Readers Theatre.

The Princess Academy by Shannon Hale

Text from pages 56–57:

Bena glared. "You were warned, Miri. Why can't you just follow the rules?"

"No one should have to follow unfair rules. We could all run home right now. We don't have to stay and put up with closets and palm lashings and insults. Our parents should know what's going on." Miri wished that she could find the right words to express her anger and fear and longing, but to her own ears her argument sounded forced.

"Don't you dare," Katar said folding her arms. "You do that they might shut down the academy and ask the priests to announce some other place as the home of the future princess. Then we'll all lose our chance because of you, Mira."

Mira stared. No one was laughing. "You really think they'll let one of us be a princess?" she asked, her voice dry and husky.

Text converted to Readers Theatre script:

A: Narrator
B: Bena
C: Mira
D: Katar
Positions: A B C D

A (Nar):   Bena glared.

B (Bena):   You were warned, Miri. Why can't you just follow the rules?

C (Mira):   No one should have to follow unfair rules. We could all run home right now. We don't have to stay and put up with closets and palm lashings and insults. Our parents should know what's going on.

A (Nar):   Miri wished that she could find the right words to express her anger and fear and longing, but to her own ears her argument sounded forced.

D (Katar):	(*Folding her arms*) Don't you dare. You do that they might shut down the academy and ask the priests to announce some other place as the home of the future princess. Then we'll all lose our chance because of you, Mira.
A (Nar):	Mira stared. No one was laughing.
C (Mira):	You really think they'll let one of us be a princess?

Commentary

As in the case of *The Penderwicks,* the conversion of *The Princess Academy* text was straightforward. All I did was assign parts for a narrator and the three characters. The only words I deleted were "she asked, her voice dry and husky" and "Katar said." I incorporated "folding her arms" as a gesture for Katar's reader. I chose this passage because it explains the circumstances of the princess academy and demonstrates the tension between Mira and the other mountain girls. I like that it provides opportunities for a dramatic opening line, a gesture, interpretation of attitude through vocal expression, and characters speaking directly to one another. Many portions of this novel would make wonderful Readers Theatre.

The Boy Who Climbed into the Moon by David Almond

Text from pages 40–41:

"I have brought some people to meet you," said Molly, "including a child with some very peculiar ideas. Say hello."

Benjamin sadly turned his eyes to them all, but said nothing.

"Stand up, dear," said Molly. "And come and have a chat."

He did as he was told. He was tall and thin and he had to stoop through the door to get into the garden.

"But you were little and curly!" said Paul.

Benjamin made no reply.

They sat on the lawn. It was warm and soft. There was a pear tree over them, with tiny new pears hanging there. The sun was slowly travelling through the sky and the shadow of the apartment block inched towards them.

"Now, then," said Molly. "How are you today?"

He said nothing.

"How *happy* are you?" she asked.

"On a scale of one to ten?" said Benjamin. His voice was very slow and very low.

"Yes, if you like," said Molly.

"Which is happy?" he said. "Is it number one or number ten?"

Molly pondered.

"Happy is ten!" she said at last.

"Ohhhhh," he groaned. "Then I am the glummest of the glum, for I am one."

"Oh, poor, poor soul," said Paul's mum and Benjamin looked at her and nodded and the tears rolled down his face and splashed down onto the grass.

"Hang on!" snapped Molly. "Silly me! I was wrong, Benjamin. Forgive me. Happy is number one!"

"Really?" said Benjamin.

"Really really really!" answered Molly.

A great transformation took place upon his face.

"Gadzooks! he said. "Then if I'm number one, it means I am happy!"

"Correct!" said Molly. "In fact, you couldn't possibly be happier!"

Benjamin clenched his fists and punched the air. He stood up and danced a jig.

Text converted to Readers Theatre script:

A: Molly
B: Paul
C: Benjamin, Paul's Dad
D: Narrator, Paul's Mum
Positions: D C B A

A (Molly): I have brought some people to meet you, including a child with some very peculiar ideas. Say hello.

D (Nar): Benjamin sadly turned his eyes to them all, but said nothing.

A (Molly): Stand up, dear. And come and have a chat.

D (Nar):   He did as he was told. He was tall and thin and he had to stoop through the door to get into the garden.

B (Paul):   But you were little and curly!

D (Nar):   Benjamin made no reply. They sat on the lawn. It was warm and soft. There was a pear tree over them, with tiny new pears hanging there. The sun was slowly travelling through the sky and the shadow of the apartment block inched towards them.

A (Molly):   Now, then. How are you today?

D (Nar):   He said nothing.

A (Molly):   How *happy* are you?

C (Benj):   On a scale of one to ten?

A (Molly):   Yes, if you like.

C (Benj):   Which is happy? Is it number one or number ten?

D (Nar):   Molly pondered.

A (Molly):   Happy is ten!

C (Benj):   Ohhhhh. Then I am the glummest of the glum, for I am one.

D (Paul's Mum): Oh, poor, poor soul.

D (Nar):   Benjamin looked at her and nodded and the tears rolled down his face and splashed down onto the grass.

A (Molly):   Hang on! Silly me! I was wrong, Benjamin. Forgive me. Happy is number one!

C (Benj):   Really?

A (Molly):   Really really really!

D (Nar):   A great transformation took place upon his face.

C (Benj):   Gadzooks! Then if I'm number one, it means I am happy!

A (Molly):   Correct! In fact, you couldn't possibly be happier!

D (Nar):   Benjamin clenched his fists and punched the air. He stood up and danced a jig.

Commentary

David Almond prepared this script for the 2010 IBBY Readers Theatre in Santiago de Compostela. The complete script is taken from one entire chapter, but this excerpt is representative of his approach. To begin, he chose a chapter that has lots of the logic-twisting humor found throughout the book. The other authors had fun reading this and the audience enjoyed it as well. His selection also introduces (in parts not included here) two other important aspects of the book: its antiwar sentiment and Paul's "crackpot idea" that the moon is really a hole in the sky. He made very few changes to the original text, mainly deleting all the speaker indicators such as "said Molly" and "answered Benjamin." He also eliminated the sentence "His voice was very slow and very low." These deletions are similar to those involved in converting *The Penderwicks* and *The Princess Academy*. What makes this conversion a bit more complicated is that it requires several actors to double up on parts. Taking multiple roles can be tricky because one actor should not have to read two parts in a row.

From Another World **by Ana Maria Machado. Translated from the Portuguese by Luisa Baeta**

Text from pages 40–41:

"Did you hear it this time?" asked Tere.

All you had to do was look at our faces to see that we had, and that it was very strange. Elisa opened her eyes wide and grabbed my arm. Leo put his finger over his mouth asking for silence.

We were quiet. I don't know for how long. But we didn't hear any more.

"It sounded like someone moving furniture. But where?" I said, just to say something and to try to get rid of that little feeling of fear you get after being startled.

"Right. It may be. But only if it's metal," said Elisa, reminding us of what we had all heard very clearly.

"Or some heavy chains being dragged," added Tere, almost in a whisper. "Like in ghost movies."

"It must have been a sound from one of the pipes. The hot water running through them sometimes makes weird noises."

"Yeah, that's right!" I agreed. "Tere isn't used to this system of water heating. It does make a lot of noise sometimes."

We were all familiar with that. A lot of the old houses used this kind of water heating. I went on explaining, "There are pipes that carry the water by the wood stove to get heated, and then they go around the rest of the house, and then . . ."

"But . . . we don't have a wood stove here, and all the heating is done by gas," interrupted Elisa.

Text converted to Readers Theatre script:

A: Mariano
B: Elisa
C: Leo
D: Tere
Positions: C B A D

D (Tere):   Did you hear it this time?

A (Mar):   All you had to do was look at our faces to see that we had, and that it was very strange. Elisa opened her eyes wide and grabbed my arm. Leo put his finger over his mouth asking for silence.

We were quiet. I don't know for how long. But we didn't hear any more.

It sounded like someone moving furniture. But where?

B (Elisa): Right. It may be. But only if it's metal.

D (Tere): (*Whispering*) Or some heavy chains being dragged. Like in ghost movies.

C (Leo): It must have been a sound from one of the pipes. The hot water running through them sometimes makes weird noises.

A (Mar): Yeah, that's right! Tere isn't used to this system of water heating. It does make a lot of noise sometimes.

We were all familiar with that. A lot of the old houses used this kind of water heating. I went on explaining, There are pipes that carry the water by the wood stove to get heated, and then they go around the rest of the house, and then . . .

B (Elisa): (*Interrupting*) But . . . we don't have a wood stove here, and all the heating is done by gas.

Commentary

This excerpt is from a script created for the 2010 IBBY Readers Theatre performance in Santiago de Compostela. We had a last-minute cast change, so I stepped in and prepared the script. Because Ana Maria Machado's novel is a ghost story, I selected a suspenseful scene that leads to the children discovering that there is a ghost in the house.

The text has four characters, so it divided naturally into four parts. As with *The Princess Academy,* converting this particular text to a script mainly involved eliminating some of the original language. I deleted "asked," "said," and "added" as well as the phrases "just to say something and to try to get rid of that little feeling of fear you get after being startled" and "reminding us of what we had all heard very clearly" because they interrupted the flow of the dialogue. I changed "almost in a whisper" and "interrupted Elisa" to directions to help the reader remember to modulate his or her voice or adjust his or her timing, thereby increasing the dramatic effect of the piece.

Igraine the Brave by Cornelia Funke

Text from page 108:

The guard had swung his horse around and looked hard at the outskirts of the forest. But the night was black as soot among the trees, and after a few endless moments the man turned away.

"Now, Igraine!" whispered the Sorrowful Knight. "Go, before his suspicions are aroused again."

"Yes, yes, I'm off," she whispered, patting Lancelot's soft muzzle one last time. "Don't worry, Lancelot, I'll be back to see you, word of knightly honor."

"Igraine!" said the Sorrowful Knight, without turning around. "If you do not disappear into that lion's mouth this minute, I'll stuff you in with my own hands!"

"All right, I've gone!" she called back softly. "But it really is a shame you won't come, too!"

By way of an answer the Sorrowful Knight only sighed.

For the second time Igraine clambered up the mane as nimbly as a squirrel. It was child's play in her feather-light suit of armor. Lancelot put his ears back anxiously and never took his eyes off her.

"Shhh!" Igraine whispered to him. "It's all right, this isn't a real mouth."

Text converted to Readers Theatre script:

A: Narrator 1 (associated with Igraine)
B: Igraine
C: Narrator 2 (associated with the Sorrowful Knight)
D: Sorrowful Knight
Positions: A B D C

C (Nar 2): The guard had swung his horse around and looked hard at the outskirts of the forest. But the night was black as soot among the trees, and after a few endless moments the man turned away again.

D (Knight): Now, Igraine! Go, before his suspicions are aroused again.

B (Igraine): Yes, yes, I'm off.

A (Nar 1): She patted Lancelot's soft muzzle one last time.

B (Igraine): Don't worry, Lancelot, I'll be back to see you, word of knightly honor.

D (Knight): Igraine! If you do not disappear into that lion's mouth this minute I'll stuff you into it with my own hands!

B (Igraine): All right, I've gone! But it really is a shame you won't come, too.

C (Nar 2): By way of an answer the Sorrowful Knight only sighed.

D (Knight): Ohhh.

A (Nar 1): For the second time Igraine clambered up the mane as nimbly as a squirrel. It was child's play in her feather-light suit of armor. Lancelot put his ears back anxiously and never took his eyes off her.

B (Igraine): Shhh! It's all right, this isn't a real mouth.

Commentary

Igraine the Brave was a bit more complicated to convert to a Readers Theatre than was *The Penderwicks, The Princess Academy, The Boy Who Climbed into the Moon,* or *From Another World.* This passage illustrates how description of action can be handled so it does not interfere with the flow of the script. Sometimes, actions such as "whispered the Sorrowful Knight" or "she called back softly" were simply eliminated. Other times, they were assigned to one of the narrators. Thus, "patting Lancelot's soft muzzle one last time" became "Igraine patted Lancelot's soft muzzle one last time." In one instance, verbalization is added to the script to dramatize the narrator's description: The Sorrowful Knight actually sighs "Ohhh" after the narrator says, "By way of answer the Sorrowful Knight only sighed."

This sample is a portion of a script used in the 2007 ALA Readers Theatre in Washington, D.C. Cornelia Funke did not mind her original words being slightly altered for the sake of the performance, and she readily suggested changes throughout the practice sessions. (See her boxed comment in chapter 5.)

Rex Zero and the End of the World by Tim Wynne-Jones

Text from pages 40–41:

It's a well-known fact that families move in the summer so that their children can wander around a new neighborhood for two months in lonely despair. You walk around the school you are going to attend in the fall wondering which window will be your new classroom and what your teacher will be like. Vulture, rhinoceros, wildcat, cow?

I patrol the chain-link fence of the schoolyard and check out the likely places I might get cornered by bullies. I don't wear funny clothes anymore and I know that *garage* rhymes with *mirage.* But I just hope that's enough.

I look at the curved archway of the entrance to the school. It's called Mutchmor. Mutchmor Public School. Like *much more* but spelled wrong and mashed together.

The school is really old. Maybe that's how people spelled in those days. Or maybe it's French. *Merci Bon Dieu.*

I've never biked past Mutchmor. It's at the corner of Lyon and Fifth, where Lyon Street ends. Fifth looks pretty run down. Diablo is always a bit nervous when we get there. But today is a lemon-pie day, complete with meringue clouds, so we decide to take the plunge. And that's when we find the pollywog pond.

The pond is off a shady backstreet down by the Rideau Canal way south of my place. And what do you know? There are kids all over this neighborhood! I pass two boys playing catch. I see a girl skipping and another couple of girls my age with hula hoops. They look at me as I go by. I wave and one of them waves back, which makes her hula hoop fall off.

Nobody is running away. A good sign.

When I see the pollywog pond, I race home to get a jar. When I get back, two boys are there. They have jars, too. I find my own stretch of weedy shore halfway around the pond. We catch about a million pollywogs between us. I hold my jar up to the light and look through the cloudy water and darting black bodies at the two boys. They are looking through their jars at me.

Text converted to Readers Theatre script:

A: Rex 1
B: Rex 2
Positions: B A

A (Rex 1): It's a well-known fact that families move in the summer so that their children can wander around a new neighborhood for two months in lonely despair. You walk around the school you are going to attend in the fall wondering which window will be your new classroom and what your teacher will be like. Vulture, rhinoceros, wildcat, cow?

B (Rex 2): I look at the curved archway of the entrance to the school. It's called Mutchmor. Mutchmor Public School. Like *much more* but spelled wrong and mashed together.

A (Rex 1): The school is really old. It's at the corner of Lyon and Fifth, where Lyon Street ends. Fifth looks pretty run down. Diablo, my trusty bike, is always a bit nervous when we get here. But today is a lemon-pie day complete with meringue clouds, so we decide to take the plunge. And that's when we find the pollywog pond.

B (Rex 2): I race home to get a jar. When I get back two boys are there. They have jars, too. I find my own stretch of weedy shoreline halfway around the pond.

Commentary

This portion of another script read at the ALA 2007 Readers Theatre in Washington, D.C., comes from a chapter titled "Movie Star Friends." A well-selected chapter can make an excellent Readers Theatre presentation, but it generally requires some cutting to accommodate a given time frame and a listener-friendly format. When he prepared this script, Tim Wynne-Jones deleted large sections of the narration to make the dialogue begin sooner than in the original text. He also combined some short paragraphs and divided the narration into two parts in a further effort to maintain the listener's attention.

In addition, he assists the listener by adding a few clarifying phrases, such as indentifying Diablo as "my trusty bike." The result is a lively piece that immediately captures the audience's attention.

Bread and Roses, Too by Katherine Paterson

Text from pages 80–81:

"Rosa? Is that you?" At least Mamma noticed she was home. Sometimes during the past week, Rosa had wondered if Mamma even knew she was alive—or cared. "Rosa, come here. We need some good schoolgirl English." Reluctantly, Rosa stood up. The floor was cold under her bare, aching feet. "Come on, quick. We need you." Then to the others, "Rosa write good as schoolteacher, eh, Rosa?" Rosa blushed to hear Mamma bragging.

"Rosina, *bambina!* Come here!" Mrs. Marino grabbed Rosa to her bosom and kissed her on both cheeks. "Growing up, you are. What grade you go to now?"

"Sixth," Rosa mumbled, embarrassed by the display.

"What she say?" Mrs. Marino asked. "I don'ta hear so good. Too much banging in the mill."

"Six," said Mamma loudly. "First in her class, too."

"That'sa fine girl," Mrs. Marino said, beaming at Rosa and kissing her again soundly. "Now, now, come, come, you sit." She turned to the women occupying the two chairs. "Up, up. Give our schoolgirl a chair." Both women stood. "No, no, not you, Mrs. Petrovsky. You got the bad legs." Mrs. Petrovsky sat down again. "Here, Rosa, right here." She put her hands on Rosa's shoulders and pushed her down on the chair nearer the table.

In front of where Rosa sat was a large white rectangle of pasteboard. Beside the pasteboard was a bottle of ink—her ink, Rosa noted, feeling a twinge of resentment that someone had dared raid her precious school supplies—and a brush about an inch wide.

Text converted to Readers Theatre script:

A: Narrator, Rosa, Mrs. Petrovsky
B: Narrator, Mamma
C: Narrator, Mrs. Marino
D: Narrator
Positions: A B C D

B (Mamma): Rosa? Is that you?

A (Nar): At least Mamma noticed she was home. Sometimes during the past week, Rosa had wondered if Mamma even knew she was alive—or cared.

B (Mamma): Rosa, come here. We need some good schoolgirl English. Come on, quick. We need you. Rosa write good as schoolteacher, eh, Rosa?

C (Mrs. M): Rosina, *bambina!* Come here!

D (Nar): Mrs. Marino grabbed Rosa to her bosom and kissed her on both cheeks.

C (Mrs. M): Growing up, you are. What grade you go to now?

A (Rosa): Sixth.

C (Mrs. M): What she say? I don'ta hear so good. Too much banging in the mill.

B (Mamma): Six! First in her class, too.

C (Mrs. M): That'sa fine girl. Now, now, come, come, you sit. Up, up. Give our schoolgirl a chair. No, no, not you, Mrs. Petrovsky. You got the bad legs. Here, Rosa, right here.

D (Nar): In front of where Rosa sat was a large white rectangle of pasteboard. Beside the pasteboard was a bottle of ink—her ink, Rosa noted, feeling a twinge of resentment that someone had dared raid her precious school supplies—and a brush about an inch wide.

Commentary

In this section of the script, which Katherine Paterson performed at the 2008 IBBY World Congress in Copenhagen, she eliminated the following phrases:

"Reluctantly, Rosa stood up. The floor was cold under her bare, aching feet."
"Then to the others,"
"Rosa blushed to hear Mamma bragging."
"Rosa mumbled, embarrassed by the display."
"Mrs. Marino asked."
"said Mamma loudly."
"Mrs. Marino said, beaming at Rosa and kissing her again soundly."
"She turned to the women occupying the two chairs."
"Both women stood."
"Mrs. Petrovsky sat down again."

Clearly, Paterson opted to delete much of the descriptive action. What she did keep ("Mrs. Marino grabbed Rosa to her bosom and kissed her on both cheeks"; "She put her hands on Rosa's shoulders and pushed her down on the chair nearer the table") adds humor and emphasis. The narrators who speak these passages are not associated with any particular character; they are available to narrate because the characters whose parts they read do not come before or after these utterances. Katherine Paterson is a master at both preparing and performing Readers Theatre scripts.

The Phantom Tollbooth by Norton Juster

Text from pages 93–95:

"Attention! Let me have your attention!" insisted the king, leaping to his feet and pounding the table. The command was entirely unnecessary, for the moment he began to speak everyone but Milo, Tock, and the distraught bug rushed from the hall, down the stairs, and out of the palace.

"Loyal subjects and friends," continued Azaz, his voice echoing in the almost empty room, "once again on this gala occasion we have—"

"Pardon me," coughed Milo as politely as possible," but everyone has gone."

"I was hoping no one would notice," said the king sadly. "It happens every time."

"They've all gone to dinner," announced the Humbug weakly, "and as soon as I catch my breath I shall join them."

'That's ridiculous. How can they eat dinner right after a banquet?" asked Milo.

"SCANDALOUS!" shouted the king. "We'll put a stop to it at once. From now on, by royal command, everyone must eat dinner before the banquet."

"But that's just as bad," protested Milo.

"You mean just as good," corrected the Humbug. "Things which are equally bad are also equally good. Try to look at the bright side of things."

Text converted to Readers Theatre script:

A: King
B: Narrator and Tock
C: Humbug
D: Milo
Positions: B C A D

A (King):   Attention! Let me have your attention!

B (Nar):	The command was entirely unnecessary, for the moment he began to speak everyone but Milo, Tock, and the Humbug rushed from the hall, down the stairs, and out of the palace.
A (King):	Loyal subjects and friends, once again on this gala occasion we have—
D (Milo):	(*cough*) Pardon me, but everyone has gone.
A (King):	I was hoping no one would notice. It happens every time.
C (Humb):	They've all gone to dinner, and just as soon as I catch my breath I shall join them.
D (Milo):	That's ridiculous. How can they eat dinner right after a banquet?
A (King):	SCANDALOUS! We'll put a stop to it at once. From now on, by royal command, everyone must eat dinner *before* the banquet!
D (Milo):	But that's just as bad.
C (Humb):	You mean just as good. Things which are equally bad are also equally good. Try to look at the bright side of things.

Commentary

In this passage, which is a portion of the script she adapted in honor of Norton Juster for the 2008 ALA Readers Theatre in Anaheim, Linda Sue Park uses much the same technique as did Katherine Paterson in the *Bread and Roses, Too* script. Park emphasizes the dialogue and quickens the pace by omitting the descriptive action. When preparing the script for our group of four readers, she carefully selected a passage that had four characters. Tock, the dog, doesn't originally have any speaking parts, but later in the passage she assigns him some lines. She also gives Tock's reader the role of narrator. The result was a delightful experience for readers and listeners, particularly audience member Norton Juster.

The Mozart Season by Virginia Euwer Wolff

Text from pages 143–144:

I'd started depending on my midnight bike rides. I saw old people walking their dogs, once a lady pushing a sleeping baby in a stroller, and I saw a man sitting on a bench in the park flossing his teeth, all alone. I saw people coming home and putting their cars in their garages, and a couple of people coming out of their houses with lunch boxes, going to work on late shifts. And the bushes and trees with their leafy shadows in the night, and once in a while a rabbit scampering in the park. One night I saw a man and lady arguing beside a tree. She said, "You always do that, every single time . . ." and he said *"You're* the one that always" something. Once I saw a porcupine in front of me on the trail, going along in its slow waddle. And usually there were cats crouching or springing, their lemon-shaped green eyes eerie in the dark. They were little stories I was seeing; they helped me get unfolded. The night riding helped me go to sleep.

But someone saw me one night and phoned my mother the next day. I heard it happen:

"*Our* Allegra? No—No. She was fast asleep in bed. You what? She *what?* Allegra, come here right now—Allegra? She—No, no. I had no idea—it was *what* time? I can't believe—Alan, come here—On her bicycle? Are you sure? Thank you, thanks. Thanks. Of course. I just didn't— Thanks, good-bye.

"Alan, you won't believe—Allegra, where were you at seven minutes after midnight last night?"

Text converted to Readers Theatre script:

A: Allegra
B: Woman, Mother
C: Father, Man
D: David (who appears later in the original script)
Podium Positions: D A C B

A (Allegra):   I'd started depending on my midnight bike rides. I saw old people walking their dogs. I saw a man sitting on a bench in the park flossing his teeth, all alone. I saw people with lunch boxes, going to work on late shifts. And the bushes and trees with their leafy shadows in the night, and once in a while a rabbit. One night I saw a man and woman arguing beside a tree.

B (Woman):   You always do that, every single time . . .

C (Man):   *You're* the one that always . . .

A (Allegra):   Once I saw a porcupine. And usually there were cats crouching or springing, their lemon-shaped green eyes eerie in the dark. They were little stories I was seeing; they helped me unfolded inside. But someone saw me one night and phoned my mother the next day. I heard it happen:

B (Mother):   *Our* Allegra? No—No. She was fast asleep in bed. You what? She *what?* Allegra, come here right now—Allegra? She—No, no. I had no idea—it was *what* time? I can't believe—Alan, come here—On her bicycle? Are you sure? Thank you, thanks. Thanks. I just didn't—

Alan, you won't believe—Allegra, where were you at seven minutes after midnight last night?

Commentary

When selecting a section from *The Mozart Season* for the 2007 ALA Readers Theatre in Washington, D.C., Virginia Euwer Wolff chose a highly dramatic scene that helps us understand the character of Allegra and the dynamics of her family. I highlight the first part of her script here to illustrate how she deleted words, phrases, clauses, and sentences not only to make the script fit our time constraints, but, more importantly, to create phrasing and cadence perfectly suited for an oral reading performance.

Gone are the images of the woman with a baby stroller, people putting their cars into garages, and details about how the rabbits and porcupine move. What remains is just enough to portray, in a manner pleasing to the ear, the importance of the midnight scenes Allegra experiences. The conversation between the man and woman remains, providing vocal texture, giving parts to other cast members, and drawing the audience more deeply into Allegra's midnight rides. Using her keen ear and strong literary sense, Virginia Euwer Wolff deftly converts one literary form into another.

Keeping Score by Linda Sue Park

Text from pages 58–59:

The radio was turned up loud enough so Mom could hear it in the kitchen. Maggie sat in the green armchair as usual, busy with score sheet and pencil. Joey-Mick lounged on the rug and plunked the ball into his glove, *thunk—thunk—thunk.* Maggie was so used to the sound that she hardly heard it. But whenever Joey-Mick stopped during an exciting play so he could concentrate on listening, she always noticed the gap in the steady beat.

As the bottom of the ninth inning approached, Maggie and Joey-Mick were both fidgeting to contain their joy. The Dodgers had scored three runs in the eighth inning to take the lead, 4–1. Just three more outs and the pennant would be theirs.

The Giants started the inning with two straight hits, followed by an out and a double that drove in a run. But just one; the Dodgers were still ahead, 4–2. Only two outs to go.

With two men on base, Bobby Thomson would be the next batter. Pitcher Ralph Branca come in to relieve starter Don Newcombe.

"Branca?" Joey-Mick exclaimed.

"It'll be okay," Maggie said immediately. She knew what Joey-Mick was thinking: In Game 1 of the playoffs, Thomson had faced Branca and hit a two-run homer. "It'll never happen twice in a row."

Joey-Mick nodded.

But if Thomson did manage to get to base, the next batter would be . . . Willie Mays. When Red Barber announced that Willie was on deck, Joey-Mick glared at Maggie so fiercely that she could feel the heat of it on the back of her neck when she bent her head down to her score sheet again.

Text converted to Readers Theatre script:

A: Narrator 1, Radio Announcer, and George
B: Narrator 2 (Maggie's Point of View) and Mom
C: Maggie
D: Narrator 3, Joey-Mick, and Terry
Positions: A B C D

A (Nar 1):   The radio was turned up loud enough so Mom could hear it in the kitchen. Maggie sat in the green armchair as usual, busy with score sheet and pencil, writing down every play just like Jim had taught her.

B (Maggie):   I bet Jim's keeping score of the game too. That's good—if I miss any plays I can get them from him later.

A (Nar 1):   Up the street at the firehouse, Jim would be rooting for the Giants, not the Dodgers. But that didn't matter when it came to keeping a score sheet: The plays were recorded the same way no matter who you were cheering for.

Joey-Mick lounged on the rug and plunked the ball into his glove, *thunk—thunk—thunk.*

B (Nar 2):   Maggie was so used to the sound that she hardly heard it. But whenever Joey-Mick stopped *thunking* during an exciting play so he could concentrate on listening, she always noticed the gap in that steady beat.

A (Nar 1):   As the bottom of the ninth inning approached, Maggie and Joey-Mick were both fidgeting to contain their joy. The Dodgers had scored three runs in the eighth inning to take the lead, 4–1. Just three more outs and the pennant would be theirs.

The Giants started the inning with two straight hits, followed by an out and a double. A run scored.

C (Maggie):   Okay, that's okay. Just one run in, we're still ahead 4–2.

D (Joey-M):   C'mon you bums, only two outs to go!

A (Nar 1):   With two men still on base, Bobby Thomson would be the next batter. Pitcher Ralph Branca came in to relieve starter Don Newcombe.

D (Joey-M):   *(in disbelief) Branca?*

C (Maggie):   It'll be okay.

B (Nar 2):   She knew what Joey-Mick was thinking: In Game 1 of the playoffs, Thomson had faced Branca and hit a two-run homer that helped the Giants win the game.

C (Maggie):   Don't worry. It'll never happen twice in a row.

D (Joey-M):   You better be right about that.

B (Nar 1):   But if Thomson did manage to get on base, the next batter would be—Willie Mays. When Red Barber announced that Willie was on deck, Joey-Mick glared at Maggie so fiercely that she could feel the heat of it on the back of her neck when she bent her head down to her score sheet again. She wouldn't look at him. She couldn't help it: Willie Mays was her favorite player even if he *was* on the wrong team.

Commentary

I used this portion of the script Linda Sue Park developed for the 2008 ALA Readers Theatre in Anaheim as an example of a text converted to script in the program notes for our Readers Theatre performance. I also included the following commentary:

> Note that Linda Sue Park both deleted from and added to the original text when she created this Readers Theatre script. She added lines to help set context by letting audience in on the relationship between Maggie and Jim, to introduce the idea of

the firehouse which will come into the script later, to provide background about Willie Mays being Maggie's favorite player, and to give Joey-Mick a chance to say "you bums," an important phrase that appears frequently in the book although not in this particular passage.

She deleted some of the baseball play details and some of the explanatory narration—such as "Joey-Mick exclaimed" and "Maggie said immediately." She also converted narration to dialogue. She changed more in the beginning of the script than she did later on. Her intent was to make sure the audience was not confused.

Converting narration to dialogue is a useful technique. It not only allows more readers to have parts, but it also provides opportunities for lively, energetic reading. Using three narrators instead of just one produces this effect as well.[1]

Kit's Wilderness by David Almond

Text from page 47:

Askew's den. The floor was damp with yesterday's rain. Water had trickled down the walls through Askew's carvings. The scent of damp, of the candles, of the bodies crouching there. Allie faced me through the flickering light. She watched me, but there was nothing in her eyes. I stared at the others, these children like me from ancient families of Stoneygate. Had something like death really happened to them: Had they really gone through something like the children on the monument? Or was it just a game and they had all pretended? I read their names.

John Askew, aged thirteen; Robert Carr, aged eleven; Wilfred Cook, aged fifteen; Dorothy Gullane, aged twelve; Alison Keenan, aged thirteen; Daniel Sharkey, aged fourteen; Louise Mc Call, aged thirteen . . .

Below them was the wide space for the names to come, and I saw my own name there, as if I was dreaming.

Christopher Watson, aged thirteen.

Text converted to Readers Theatre script:

A: Kit (Christopher Watson)
B: Allie (Alison Keenan)
C: Askew
D: Narrator, Other
Positions: D A B C

D (Nar): The floor was damp with yesterday's rain. Water had trickled down the walls through Askew's carvings. The scent of damp, of the candles, of the bodies crouching there.

A (Kit): Allie faced me through the flickering light. She watched me, but there was nothing in her eyes. I stared at the others, these children like me from the ancient families of Stoneygate. Had something like death really happened to them? Had they really gone through something like the children on the monument? Or was it just a game and they had all pretended? I read their names.

C (Askew): John Askew, aged thirteen;

D (Other): Robert Carr, aged eleven;
Dorothy Gullane, aged twelve;
Wilfred Cook, aged fifteen;
Daniel Sharkey, aged fourteen;
Louise Watson, aged thirteen . . .

B (Allie): Alison Keenan, aged thirteen.

A (Kit): Below them was the wide space for the names to come, and I saw my own name there, as if I were dreaming.
Christopher Watson, aged thirteen.

Commentary

David Almond converted this text into a script for the 2007 ALA Readers Theatre in Washington, D.C. This entire passage is actually written in first-person narrative. However, Almond divided the narrator's role among the readers, always assigning the same reader parts related to the same character. This division not only provided parts for all four readers, but it also ensured lively pacing and energetic interaction among the readers. The author also deleted phrases such as "he whispered" and "we all chanted" and eliminated some of the description or assigned it to the narrator.

It was dramatic having Askew, Allie, and Kit read their own names among those of the dead inscribed on the monument in Askew's den. Changing the order of the names on the wall so that Allie read her name last was particularly effective. The changes Almond made evoked an even more eerie and ghostly atmosphere than did the original text.

I included this portion of David Almond's script and a version of the above commentary in the program notes for the 2007 IBBY Regional in Tucson, where he read the script with members of the USBBY executive board.[2]

The Astonishing Life of Octavian Nothing, Traitor to the Nation by M. T. Anderson

Text from page 5:

The men who raised me were lords of matter, and in the dim chambers I watched as they traced the spinning of bodies celestial in vast, iron courses, and bid sparks to dance upon their hands; they read the bodies of fish as if each dying trout or shad was a fresh Biblical Testament, the wet and twitching volume of a new-born Pentateuch. They burned holes in the air, wrote poems of love, sucked the venom from sores, painted landscapes of gloom, and made metal sing; they dissected fire like newts.

Text converted to Readers Theatre script.

A: Octavian 1, Girl
B: Octavian 2
C: Octavian 3, Gitney (Mr. 03–01)
D: Octavian 4, Mother
Podium Positions: A B C D

A (O#1):   In that gaunt house lived many men, lords of matter; and in its many rooms they read their odes, or played the violin, or performed their philosophical exercises. They combined chemical compounds and stirred them.

C (O#3):   They cut apart birds to trace the structure of the avian skeleton.

D (O#4):   Masked in leather hoods, they dissected a skunk.

B (O#2):   They kept cages full of fireflies. They coaxed reptiles with mice.

A (O#1):   They bade sparks to dance upon their hands; they burned holes in the air, wrote poems of love, sucked the venom from sores, painted landscapes of gloom, and made metal sing; they dissected fire like newts.

Commentary

Octavian Nothing, Traitor to the Nation is the most ambitious text we have used in our Readers Theatre presentations. M. T. (Tobin) Anderson rose to the challenge brilliantly when he prepared its script for the 2008 ALA Readers Theatre in Anaheim.

As can be seen in the excerpt, the original text is primarily written from the first-person point of view. Anderson broke up Octavian's narrative into four parts and assigned one to each reader. In an effort to convey the gist of the story line in the complete script, he eliminated long descriptive sections and inserted paraphrased portions from other sections of the novel. (These changes are not shown here due to their complexity.)

Anderson's substantial changes required deep understanding of the plot and the ability to maintain the integrity of the piece by writing in the author's style. Of course, as the author, he had both these qualifications. The process, however, was multiphased, and he continued to delete passages throughout each rehearsal session.

Novels in Verse

Novels in verse come in a variety of forms. Some, of course, lend themselves more readily to Readers Theatre than others. Some novels in verse provide multiple perspectives from alternating narrators. These works can be performed by one reader taking one character's part and reading only that. Thus, if there are six characters in the novel, there would be six readers in the Readers Theatre troupe. (See suggestions for using this type of format under the entry for Andrea Cheng's *Where the Steps Were* in chapter 8.) Other novels in verse consist of a series of poems that combine to tell a story from one character's perspective. It is a bit complicated to divide an individual character's part among several readers because the wording in a novel in verse should probably not be altered by eliminating speaker identifiers. The following examples demonstrate how this might be accomplished.

Brushing Mom's Hair **by Andrea Cheng**

Text from page 7:

Ballet

We stretch,
thin arms
touching toes.
Linda says,
Can you believe
my mom's friend
had one of her breasts
cut off?
Becky covers her mouth
with her hand.
Really?
I look at them
in the mirror,
eyebrows raised,
eyes open
wide.

I bend
and touch my forehead
to my knee.
I don't say,
My mom
had both her breasts cut off
and now she has stitches
covered by bandages
where they were.

Text converted to Readers Theatre script:

A: Ann narrator
B: Ann dialogue
C: Linda
D: Becky
Positions: C A B D

D (Becky):   Ballet

A (Ann nar):   We stretch,
thin arms
touching toes.
Linda says,

C (Linda):   Can you believe
my mom's friend
had one of her breasts
cut off?

A (Ann nar):   Becky covers her mouth
with her hand.

D (Becky):   *Really?*

A (Ann nar):   I look at them
in the mirror,
eyebrows raised,

eyes open
wide.
I bend
and touch my forehead
to my knee.
I don't say,

B (Ann dia):   My mom
had both her breasts cut off
and now she has stitches
covered by bandages
where they were.

Commentary

When performing a novel written in verse as Readers Theatre, it is tempting to have each reader read a whole poem, particularly if the poem is basically from one character's perspective—as this one is from Ann's. But rather than do this, I divided the poem into four parts. Since Ann, as narrator, was reporting what she and the others said, it was natural to let the three of them speak for themselves by assigning each of their parts to a different reader. The title is an important part of the poem, so one of the readers announces it. This poem begins the story of Ann and her mother's journey through breast cancer. A series of well-selected poems from the remainder of the book can readily convey the story line.

This Full House by Virginia Euwer Wolff

Text from pages 362–363:

And then Ricky announces about Jeremy:
"This boy can read words,
but he never hit a ball with a bat,
we gotta change that."
I was to be at Jolly's by 8:00 a.m. on a Saturday,
but when I get there
Ricky's training class has been delayed,

so he brings out a lightweight ball,
a small lightweight bat,
and a batter's helmet to fit that little head I love so much,
and we are going to the park.
Jolly says, "I'm his mother,
I have to be there if he hits a ball,
I'm goin' too."
So she carries a book to study if she decides to study,
she won't look at me or talk to me,
she keeps at least one child between us,
we all walk in a bunch on such a clear morning
with such blue sky
it seems everybody in the world
should have some hope today. Some. Small.
One addict even smiled at us as we passed by.
Jeremy figures out front and back of the helmet,
and Ricky begins to show him how to hold the bat.
So far, so good.
But Jeremy has a hard time finding the ball in the air
and the bat doesn't get near it. Not even near.
Maybe it's his eyes? His glasses?
Pitch, swing,
pitch, swing,
pitch, swing.

Text converted to Readers Theatre script:

A: LaVaughn
B: Ricky
C: Jolly
D: Jeremy and Jilly
Podium Positions: C D A B

A (LaV)   And then Ricky announces about Jeremy:

B (Ricky):   This boy can read words,
                 but he never hit a ball with a bat,
                 we gotta change that.

A (LaV):   I was to be at Jolly's by 8:00 a.m. on a Saturday,
but when I get there

B (Ricky):   Ricky's training class has been delayed,
so he brings out a lightweight ball,
a small lightweight bat,
and a batter's helmet

A (LaV):   to fit that little head I love so much,
and we are going to the park. Jolly says,

C (Jolly):   I'm his mother,
I have to be there if he hits a ball,
I'm goin' too.

A (LaV):   So she carries a book to study if she decides to study,
she won't look at me or talk to me,
she keeps at least one child between us,
we all walk in a bunch on such a clear morning
with such blue sky
it seems everybody in the world
should have some hope today. Some. Small.

B (Ricky):   One addict even smiled at us as we passed by.
Jeremy figures out front and back of the helmet,
and Ricky begins to show him how to hold the bat.
So far, so good.
But Jeremy has a hard time finding the ball in the air
and the bat doesn't get near it. Not even near.
Maybe it's his eyes? His glasses?

D (Jeremy):   Pitch, swing,
pitch, swing,
pitch, swing.

Commentary

This passage was performed by the 2007 ALA Readers Theatre troupe in Washington, D.C. In preparing the script, Virginia Euwer Wolff had an interesting challenge. Much of the narrative comes from LaVaughn's per-spective and in her voice, but Wolff had a cast of four authors who needed roughly equal parts. To meet the challenge, she selected a scene that was relatively self-contained and had five characters present. She gracefully infused appropriate voices into LaVaughn's narrative and revised line breaks, all without interrupting the flow or pace of her meticulously se-lected words. By leaving the words exactly as she wrote them, she did not risk altering the gentle rhythms that make the passage (and the book as a whole) a superb auditory pleasure. Although it was tricky to get the pacing precisely right, the group rehearsed earnestly and, in the end, performed the piece masterfully. The author's intimacy with her text, which was a work in progress at the time, was invaluable in this situation. I learned much from her.

Out of the Dust by Karen Hesse

Text from pages 83 and 84:

The Path of Our Sorrow

Miss Freeland said,
"During the Great War we fed the world.
We couldn't grow enough wheat
to fill all the bellies.
The price the world paid for our wheat
was so high
it swelled our wallets
and our heads,
and we bought bigger tractors,
more acres,
until we had mortgages,
and rent,
and bills,
beyond reason,
but we all felt so useful, we didn't notice.

Then the war ended and before long,
Europe didn't need our wheat anymore,
they could grow their own.
But we needed Europe's money
to pay our mortgage,
our rent,
our bills.
We squeezed more cattle,
more sheep,
onto less land,
and they grazed down the stubble
till they reached root.
And the price of wheat kept dropping
so we had to grow more bushels
to make the same amount of money we made before,
to pay for all that equipment, all that land,
and the more sod we plowed up,
the drier things got,
because the water that used to collect there
under the grass,
biding its time,
keeping things alive through the dry spells
wasn't there anymore.
Without the sod the water vanished,
the soil turned to dust.
Until the wind took it,
lifting it up and carrying it away.
Such a sorrow doesn't come suddenly,
there are a thousand steps to take
before you get there."
But now,
sorrow climbs up our front steps,
big as Texas, and we didn't even see it coming,
even though it'd been making its way straight for us
all along.
September 1934

Text converted to Readers Theatre script:

A: Billie Jo, Miss Freeland 4
B: Miss Freeland 1
C: Miss Freeland 2
D: Miss Freeland 3
Podium Positions: C A B D

C (MF3):	*September 1934* The Path of Our Sorrow
A (BJ):	Miss Freeland said,
B (MF1):	During the Great War we fed the world.
C (MF2):	We couldn't grow enough wheat to fill all the bellies.
D (MF3):	The price the world paid for our wheat was so high it swelled our wallets
A (MF4):	and our heads,
B (MF1):	and we bought bigger tractors,
C (MF2):	more acres,
D (MF3):	until we had mortgages,
A (MF4):	and rent,
B (MF1):	and bills,
C (MF2):	beyond reason,
D (MF3):	but we all felt so useful, we didn't notice.

A (MF4):   Then the war ended and before long,
            Europe didn't need our wheat anymore,

B (MF1):   they could grow their own.

C: (MF2):   But we needed Europe's money
            to pay our mortgage,

D (MF3):   our rent,

A (MF4):   our bills.

B (MF1):   We squeezed more cattle,

C (MF2):   more sheep,

D (MF3):   onto less land,

A (MF4):   and they grazed down the stubble
            till they reached root.

B (MF1):   And the price of wheat kept dropping
            so we had to grow more bushels

C: (MF2):   to make the same amount of money we made before,

D (MF3):   to pay for all that equipment, all that land,

A (MF4):   and the more sod we plowed up,
            the drier things got,

B (MF1):   because the water that used to collect there
            under the grass,

C (MF2):   biding its time,

D (MF3):   keeping things alive through the dry spells

A, B, C, D (all):   wasn't there anymore.

A (MF4):   Without the sod the water vanished,

B (MF1):   the soil turned to dust.

C (MF2):   Until the wind took it,

D (MF3):   lifting it up and carrying it away.

B (MF1):   Such a sorrow doesn't come suddenly,
there are a thousand steps to take
before you get there.

A (BJ):   But now,
sorrow climbs up our front steps,
big as Texas, and we didn't even see it coming,
even though it'd been making its way straight for us
all along.

Commentary

Although this excerpt has only two speakers, I made it have four for the sake of variety and emphasis. This modification works well in a self-contained, free-verse passage such as this because it is the words that matter, not the speaker. Since the title and date are important to the context of the passage, I had them announced in the beginning. So many speaker changes will require much practice in order to get Karen Hesse's impeccable timing and pacing exactly right, but the result will be well worth the effort.

Poetry

The difference between a poetry reading and a Readers Theatre poetry presentation is that in Readers Theatre each poem is presented by more than one reader. The Readers Theatre program may consist completely of poetry, or it may be a combination of various literary forms. The following poems, one from a collection based on a specific poetic form and two from themed collections, illustrate how poetry can be converted to Readers Theatre scripts.

Tap Dancing on the Roof by Linda Sue Park

Poem from page 7 of unpaged book:

October

The wind rearranges the leaves,
As if to say, "Much better *there,*"
and coaxes others off their trees:
"It's lots more fun in the air."
Then it plays tag with a plastic bag,
And with one gust uncombs my hair!

Poem converted to Readers Theatre script.

A: Narrator 1
B: Wind
C: Narrator 2
Positions: A B C

C (Nar 2):   October

A (Nar 1):   The wind rearranges the leaves,
                As if to say,

B (Wind):   Much better *there,*

A (Nar 2):   and coaxes others off their trees:

B (Wind):   It's lots more fun in the air.

C (Nar 2):   Then it plays tag with a plastic bag,
                And with one gust uncombs my hair!

Commentary
Although written from one point of view, this poem has clear possibilities
for involving several readers. This poem is actually a *sijo,* a traditional Korean form of poetry with strict syllabic structure. Because each *sijo* is com-

posed of three lines (or sentences) it naturally lends itself to being read by three readers. In the case of "October," rather than assign roles according to sentence structure, I gave the wind its own voice and divided the rest between two narrators.

Dizzy in Your Eyes: Poems About Love by Pat Mora

Poem from page 7:

I Can Dance

I can dance,
moving muscles and knees,
shoulders and hips,
smart as you please.
came out of rhyme.
I can dance,
like the guys on TV,
like the dudes on the street,
feeling free and at ease.
I can dance,
the old and the new,
baby, I've got the beat.
Watch my steps. It's a breeze—

in my room alone
with the door closed.

Poem converted to Readers Theatre script:

A: Narrator 1
B: Narrator 2
C: Narrator 3
Positions: C A B

All (Nars 1, 2, 3): I Can Dance

A (Nar 1):   I can dance,
moving muscles and knees,
shoulders and hips,
smart as you please.
came out of rhyme.

B (Nar 2):   I can dance,
like the guys on TV,
like the dudes on the street,
feeling free and at ease.

C (Nar 3):   I can dance,
the old and the new,
baby, I've got the beat.
Watch my steps. It's a breeze—

All (Nars 1, 2, 3): (*Whispering*)
in my room alone
with the door closed.

Commentary

Although there is only one voice in this poem, I assigned parts for three readers. Having all three readers announce the title and whisper the last lines in unison emphasizes the commonality of an experience to which many teens may relate.

Central Heating: Poems About Fire and Warmth by Marilyn Singer

Poem from page 4:

Contradiction

Fire has contradiction
at its heart,
from that wintery blue part
to its jagged golden crown.

It gives comfort
in a candle's cozy flickering.
It brings terror
in a forest's burning down.
It is both the bolt of lightening
that splits a summer sky
and the burst of July fireworks
that unites a wide-eyed town.
From its smoldering end
to its sudden start,
Fire has contradiction
at its heart.

Poem converted to Readers Theatre script:

A: Narrator 1
B: Narrator 2
C: Narrator 3
D: Narrator 4

A (Nar 1):   Contradiction

All (Nars 1, 2, 3, 4): Fire has contradiction
at its heart,

B (Nar 2):   from that wintery blue part

C (Nar 3):   to its jagged golden crown.

D (Nar 4):   It gives comfort
in a candle's cozy flickering.

A (Nar 1):   It brings terror
in a forest's burning down.

B (Nar 2):   It is both the bolt of lightening
that splits a summer sky

C (Nar 3):   and the burst of July fireworks
              that unites a wide-eyed town.

D (Nar 4):   From its smoldering end

B (Nar 2):   to its sudden start,

All (Nars 1, 2, 3, 4): Fire has contradiction
              at its heart.

Commentary

Dividing the main ideas of the poem among four readers highlights the various aspects of fire mentioned in the poem. Having all four readers read the first and last lines together emphasizes the poet's point that fire is the sum of all its contradictory parts.

Story Collections

Story collections come in all sizes and cover all topics. Some collections contain several stories written by the same author. Sometimes these stories contain a common theme or thread, sometimes they don't. Others are themed collections of stories written by various authors about a particular topic or idea. Some are folktales, some are contemporary stories, some are fantasies, some are science fiction, some are historical. They are written for and enjoyed by all level readers. Their length, focus, and wide variety of subject matter make story collections fertile ground for Readers Theatre.

"Shotgun Cheatham's Last Night Above Ground" by Richard Peck. In *Twelve Shots: Outstanding Short Stories About Guns,* edited by Harry Mazer

Text from page 125:

"Down at The Coffee Pot they say Shotgun rode with the James boys."
"Which James boys?" Grandma asked.
"Jesse James," I said, "and Frank."

"They wouldn't have had him," she said. "Anyhow, those James were Missouri People."

"They were telling the reporter Shotgun killed a man and went to the penitentiary."

"Several around here done that," Grandma said, "though I don't recall him being out of town any length of time. Who's doing all this talking?"

"A real old, humped-over lady with buck teeth," Mary Alice said.

"Cross-eyed?" Grandma said. "That'd be Effie Wilcox. You think she's ugly now, you should have seen her as a girl. And she'd talk you to death. Her tongue's attached in the middle and flaps at both ends." Grandma was over by the screen door for a breath of air.

"They said he'd notched his gun in six places," I said, pushing my luck.

"They said the notches were either for banks he'd robbed or for sheriffs he'd shot."

"Was that Effie again? Never trust an ugly woman. She's got a grudge against the world," said Grandma, who was no oil painting herself. She fetched up a sigh. "I'll tell you how Shotgun got his name."

Text converted to Readers Theatre script:

A: Boy
B: Grandma
C: Mary Alice
D: Narrator
Positions: C A B D

A (Boy):   Down at The Coffee Pot they say Shotgun rode with the James boys.

B (Gma):   Which James boys?

A (Boy):   Jesse James and Frank.

B (Gma):   They wouldn't have had him. Anyhow, those James were Missouri People.

A (Boy):   They were telling the reporter Shotgun killed a man and went to the penitentiary.

B (Gma):   Several around here done that, though I don't recall him being out of town any length of time. Who's doing all this talking?

C (Mary A):   A real old, humped-over lady with buck teeth.

B (Gma):   Cross-eyed? That'd be Effie Wilcox. You think she's ugly now, you should have seen her as a girl. And she'd talk you to death. Her tongue's attached in the middle and flaps at both ends.

D (Nar):   Grandma was over by the screen door for a breath of air.

A (Boy):   They said he'd notched his gun in six places. They said the notches were either for banks he'd robbed or for sheriffs he'd shot.

B (Gma):   Was that Effie again? Never trust an ugly woman. She's got a grudge against the world.

D (Nar):   Grandma was no oil painting herself.

B (Gma):   *(Sighing)* I'll tell you how Shotgun got his name.

Commentary

This short story would need very little revision to convert it to a Readers Theatre script. For this portion, I merely eliminated expressions such as "he said" and "she said" and a small amount of description. I considered leaving out the part about Grandma standing by the door but decided to leave it in to introduce the voice of the narrator. Likewise, I could have left out the description of Grandma not being an oil painting herself, but assigning it to the narrator as an isolated line underscores the ironic humor of the piece.

Writing this short story for this themed collection on guns inspired Richard Peck to write *A Long Way from Chicago,* which won a Newbery

Honor; its sequel, *A Year Down Yonder,* which won a Newbery Medal; and its companion, *A Season of Gifts.* In and out of Readers Theatre, short stories can lead to great happenings.

Nonfiction

As with most literary genres, there is a place for nonfiction in Readers Theatre. I've included three examples that demonstrate how this can be done: two from exceptionally well-written historical nonfiction works that use a traditional format (text illustrated with photographs) and one from a spectacularly well-executed autobiographical work that uses a nontraditional picture book format. The first, which is about the 1845 Irish potato famine, might work well with scripts developed from historical fiction dealing with the same event. The second, which documents the role children and teens played in the civil rights movement, might work well with other texts about civil rights or Martin Luther King Jr. Either book could be used as part of an author-focused Readers Theatre performance that includes several selections from Susan Campbell Bartoletti's or Elizabeth Partridge's other works of nonfiction. The third, Peter Sís's masterpiece, could be extended to be a performance in itself. However they are used, these award-winning works illustrate that nonfiction can be transposed into captivating Readers Theatre.

Black Potatoes: The Story of the Great Irish Potato Famine, 1845–1850 by Susan Campbell Bartoletti

Text from page 5–6:

The weather in Ireland has always been fickle, but the weather during the summer of 1845 was worse than the oldest people could remember. First the July days burned hot, much hotter than usual. After several days, the hot spell ended and the weather turned gloomy, cold, and damp. For three weeks in August, heavy rains fell every day.

The changeable weather made some uneasy. They had heard reports about potato fields that had blackened overnight in some parts of Ireland. They watched their crops for signs of decay, but the plants appeared to be thriving, with their tiny purple flowers, large flat green leaves, and sturdy stalks. The people couldn't see the potatoes, which grew on stems beneath the ground, but they prayed that the tubers were swelling, large and round.

Text converted into Readers Theatre script:

A: Narrator 1
B: Narrator 2
C: Narrator 3
D: Narrator 4
Positions: A C B D

A (Nar 1): The weather in Ireland has always been fickle, but the weather during the summer of 1845 was worse than the oldest people could remember.

B (Nar 2): First the July days burned hot, much hotter than usual. After several days, the hot spell ended and the weather turned gloomy, cold, and damp. For three weeks in August, heavy rains fell every day.

C (Nar 3): The changeable weather made some uneasy. They had heard reports about potato fields that had blackened overnight in some parts of Ireland.

D (Nar 4): They watched their crops for signs of decay, but the plants appeared to be thriving, with their tiny purple flowers, large flat green leaves, and sturdy stalks. The people couldn't see the potatoes, which grew on stems beneath the ground, but they prayed that the tubers were swelling, large and round.

Commentary

The fluidity of the narrative makes this text easy to read aloud. Chunking the related ideas for each narrator to read provides variety for listeners. The four voices create a communal effect that emphasizes the far-reaching seriousness of the situation and elicits the audience's sympathy and curiosity.

Marching for Freedom: Walk Together, Children, and Don't You Grow Weary **by Elizabeth Partridge**

Text from page 1:

> The first time Joanne Blackmon was arrested, she was just ten years old.
>
> After breakfast one morning, she and her grandmother, Sylvia Johnson, left their apartment in the Carver Homes in Selma, Alabama. Mrs. Johnson walked purposefully down Sylvan Street, turning onto Alabama Street for the six short blocks to the downtown shopping area. Mrs. Johnson intended to register to vote. She knew she wouldn't be allowed to. It was almost impossible for blacks to register. But she wanted to show white authorities that she, like all Americans, deserved the right to vote.

Text converted to Readers Theatre script:

A: Narrator 1
B: Narrator 2
C: Narrator 3
D: Narrator 4
Positions: A B C D

A (Nar 1):   The first time Joanne Blackmon was arrested, she was just ten years old.

B (Nar 2):   After breakfast one morning, she and her grandmother, Sylvia Johnson, left their apartment in the Carver Homes in Selma, Alabama.

C (Nar 3):   Mrs. Johnson walked purposefully down Sylvan Street, turning onto Alabama Street for the six short blocks to the downtown shopping area.

D (Nar 4):   Mrs. Johnson intended to register to vote.

B (Nar 2):   She knew she wouldn't be allowed to.

A (Nar 1):   It was almost impossible for blacks to register.

C (Nar 3):   But she wanted to show white authorities that she, like all Americans,

ALL: deserved the right to vote.

Commentary

The details of Joanne's and her grandmother's walk immediately draw readers in, making us feel as if we are walking with them down Sylvan Street. I signify the importance of the details by assigning each line to a separate narrator. The last phrase, however, is spoken by all the narrators to emphasize the *all* in all Americans and to the show the unity that was needed to overcome the tremendous barriers placed in the way of black people who were trying to register to vote.

The Wall: Growing Up Behind the Iron Curtain by Peter Sís

Text and images from pages 1–3 of unpaged text:

As long as he could remember, he had loved to draw.

As long as he could remember, he had loved to draw.

IRON CURTAIN: The boundary that symbolically, ideologically, and physically divided Europe into two separate areas after World War II.

COLD WAR: The geopolitical, ideological, and economic struggle that emerged between capitalism and communism from 1945 to 1991.

COMMUNISM: The ideology of the Soviet Union and other countries; a system of government in which the state controls all social and economic activity.

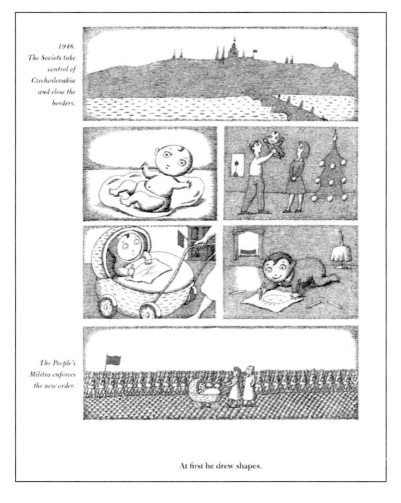

At first he drew shapes.

1948: The Soviets take control of Czechoslovakia and close the borders.

The People's Militia enforces the new order.

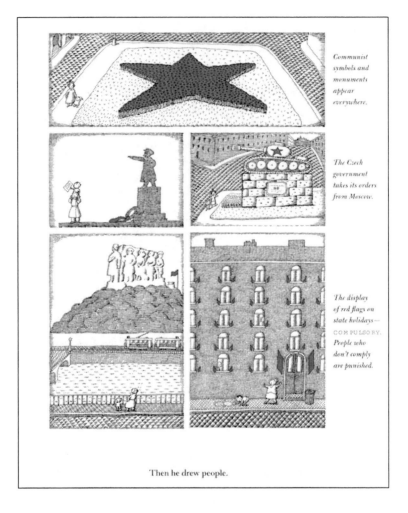

Communist symbols and monuments appear everywhere.

The Czech government takes its orders from Moscow.

The display of red flags on state holidays— COMPULSORY. People who don't comply are punished.

Then he drew people.

Then he drew people.

Communist symbols and monuments appear everywhere.

The Czech government takes its orders from Moscow.

The display of red flags on state holidays—COMPULSORY. People who don't comply are punished.

Text converted to Readers Theatre script:

A: Boy
B: Narrator 1
C: Narrator 2
D: Narrator 3
Positions: B A C D

A (Boy):   As long as he could remember, he had loved to draw.

B (Nar 1):   Iron Curtain: The boundary that symbolically, ideologically, and physically divided Europe into two separate areas after World War II.

C (Nar 2):   Cold War: The geopolitical, ideological, and economic struggle between capitalism and communism from 1945 to1991.

D (Nar 3):   Communism: The ideology of the Soviet Union and other countries; a system of government in which the state controls all social and economic activity.

A (Boy):   At first he drew shapes.

C (Nar 2):   1948. The Soviets take control of Czechoslovakia.

B (Nar 1):   The People's Militia enforces the new order.

A (Boy):   Then he drew people.

D (Nar 3):   Communist symbols and monuments appear everywhere.

C (Nar 2):   The Czech government takes its orders from Moscow.

B (Nar 1):   The display of red flags on state holidays—COMPULSORY. People who do not comply are punished.

Commentary

Contrasting vocal expressions are key to a Readers Theatre performance of *The Wall*. As the boy fluidly and expressively tells his story about loving art and freedom, the narrators solemnly relate the rigid control imposed on his country by the Soviet government. Although the script dealt only with verbal aspects of this multilayered, uniquely formatted, and intricately complex picture book, our audience at the 2008 IBBY World Congress in Copenhagen was riveted.

Those international educators familiar with the book were amazed that it could be transposed into a minimalist dramatic performance such as our Readers Theatre. Those unfamiliar with the book will, I suspect, be reading it soon. They will see that we had to be selective about which captions to include along with the boy's narrative. Our collaborative efforts during rehearsals made the script exceptional. Not surprisingly, given the nature of the book and the authors in our group, including Peter Sís and Katherine Paterson, the performance was a joyful celebration of freedom, creativity, and all the arts.

Notes

1. Elizabeth A. Poe. Unpublished program notes for "Creating Readers Theatre at Your Library with Top Quality Children's Books: A Performance in Five Acts and an Intermission." ALA annual conference, Washington, D.C., June 28, 2008. Pp. 5–6.
2. Elizabeth A. Poe. Unpublished program notes for "Coal Mining, Readers Theatre, and David Almond's *Kit's Wilderness.*" IBBY regional conference, Tucson, Arizona, Nov. 3, 2007. Pp. 3–4.

Resources

Almond, David. *The Boy Who Climbed into the Moon*. Illus. by Polly Dunbar. Somerville, MA: Candlewick, 2010. (Originally published in England by Walker, 2010.)

———. *Kit's Wilderness*. New York: Delacorte, 2000. (Originally published in Great Britain by Hodder, 1999.)

Anderson, M. T. *The Astonishing Life of Octavian Nothing, Traitor to the Nation. Vol. 1: The Pox Party*. Cambridge, MA: Candlewick, 2006.

Bartoletti, Susan Campbell. *Black Potatoes: The Story of the Great Irish Famine, 1845–1850*. Boston: Houghton Mifflin, 2001.

Birdsall, Jeanne. *The Penderwicks: A Summer Tale of Four Sisters, Two Rabbits, and a Very Interesting Boy*. New York: Knopf, 2005.

Burton, Virginia Lee. *Mike Mulligan and His Steam Shovel.* Illus. by author. Boston: Houghton Mifflin, 1939.

Cheng, Andrea. *Brushing Mom's Hair.* Illus. by Nicole Wong. Honesdale, PA: Wordsong, 2009.

Funke, Cornelia. *Igraine the Brave.* Trans. by Anthea Bell. New York: Chicken House/Scholastic, 2007. (Originally published in Germany by Cecilie Dressler, 1998.)

Hesse, Karen. *Out of the Dust.* New York: Scholastic, 1997.

Juster, Norton. *The Phantom Tollbooth.* Illus. by Jules Feiffer. New York: Knopf, 1964. (Originally published by Epstein and Carroll, 1961.)

Kvasnosky, Laura McGee. *Zelda and Ivy: The Runaways.* Cambridge, MA: Candlewick, 2006.

Machado, Ana Maria. *From Another World.* Illus. by Lúcia Brandão. Trans. by Luisa Baeta. Toronto: Groundwood, 2005. (Originally published in Brazil by Editora Ática, 2002.)

Mahy, Margaret. *Bubble Trouble.* Illus. by Polly Dunbar. New York: Clarion, 2009.

Mazer, Harry. *Twelve Shots: Outstanding Short Stories About Guns.* New York: Delacorte, 1997.

Mora, Pat. *Dizzy in Your Eyes: Poems About Love.* New York: Knopf, 2010.

Park, Linda Sue. *Tap Dancing on the Roof.* Illus. by Istvan Banyai. New York: Clarion, 2007.

———. *Keeping Score.* New York: Clarion, 2008.

Partridge, Elizabeth. *Marching for Freedom: Walk Together, Children, and Don't You Grow Weary.* New York: Viking, 2009.

Paterson, Katherine. *Bread and Roses, Too.* New York: Clarion, 2006.

———. *Marvin One Too Many.* Illus. by Jane Clark Brown. New York: HarperCollins, 2001.

———. *The Same Stuff as Stars.* New York: Clarion, 2002.

Peck, Richard. *A Long Way from Chicago.* New York: Dial, 1998.

———. *A Season of Gifts.* New York: Dial, 2009.

———. *A Year Down Yonder.* New York: Dial, 2000.

———. "Shotgun Cheatham's Last Night Above Ground." In *Twelve Shots: Outstanding Short Stories About Guns,* edited by Harry Mazer. New York: Delacorte, 1997.

Poe, Elizabeth A. *BookNotes Educators Guide for The Penderwicks: A Summer Tale of Four Sisters, Two Rabbits, and a Very Interesting Boy by Jeanne Birdsall.* New York: Random House, 2007.

———. Unpublished program notes for "Coal Mining, Readers Theatre, and David Almond's *Kit's Wilderness.*" IBBY regional conference, Tucson, Arizona, Nov. 3. 2007.

————. Unpublished program notes for "Creating Readers Theatre at Your Library with Top Quality Children's Books: A Performance in Five Acts and an Intermission." ALA Annual Conference, Washington, D.C., June 28, 2008.

Rohmann, Eric. *A Kitten Tale*. New York: Knopf, 2008.

Sierra, Judy. *Wild About Books*. Illus. by Marc Brown. New York: Knopf, 2004.

Singer, Marilyn. *Central Heating: Poems About Fire and Warmth*. Illus. by Meilo So. New York: Knopf, 2005.

Sís, Peter. *The Wall: Growing Up Behind the Iron Curtain*. New York: Frances Foster/Farrar Straus Giroux, 2007.

Wolff, Virginia Euwer. *This Full House*. New York: The Bowen Press/Harper Teens, 2009.

Wynne-Jones, Tim. *Rex Zero and the End of the World*. New York: Melanie Kroupa/Farrar Straus Giroux, 2007. (Originally published in Canada by Groundwood, 2006.)

Pre-Performance Preparation

Sample Timelines for Planning a Readers Theatre Experience

THE FOLLOWING FOUR TIMELINES ARE DESIGNED TO ASSIST LIBRARIANS, teachers, and other adults interested in facilitating Readers Theatre experiences in libraries. The timetables, which are geared toward different age groups, are general in hopes that facilitators will adapt them to their specific situations. To this end, I am calling them timelines rather than lesson plans or programming procedures. These timelines are meant to supplement information in chapters 1 through 5 of this book and to be used in extracurricular situations.

Context

Your library has been invited to participate in National Library Week in April. The purpose is to raise awareness of the importance of libraries in the community. You will be contributing to this public service effort by coordinating a Readers Theatre performance your library. Children and teens from kindergarten to high school ages will be involved either as readers or audience members. You will serve as program director.

A call for volunteers has attracted a group of nineteen children and teens interested in participating in the project. The group has agreed to work together to prepare and present a Readers Theatre performance using books about libraries. The title of the performance will be "Libraries in Books." The performance will consist of four readings done by four different groups of readers. Each group will work with you or another adult facilitator to prepare and practice its script. The whole group, or troupe, will practice together before giving the performance in April. One of the older teen volunteers will be your assistant program director.

Meeting schedules and agendas for each group will vary within the six-week period designated as preparation time, but the troupe as a whole has a common goal: to plan and perform a Readers Theatre program titled "Libraries in Books."

Books to Consider

Library Lion by Michelle Knudsen
When a lion enters the library, he is allowed to stay as long as he doesn't break any rules.

> *Sample passage:*
> One day, a lion come to the library. He walked right past the circulation desk and up into the stacks. *(p. 2 of unpaged book)*

The Librarian and the Robbers by Margaret Mahy
A band of robbers kidnap the town's librarian but end up loving books and eventually becoming librarians themselves.

> *Sample passage:*
> So, ever after, that particular library was remarkably well run. With all the extra librarians they suddenly had, the council was able to open a children's library with story readings and adventure plays every day. The robber librarians had become very good at such things practicing around their campfires in the forest. *(p. 71)*

Tomás and the Library Lady by Pat Mora

Tomás and his family are migrant workers. Assisted by the town's friendly public librarian, he discovers the world of books. This book is based on a true story.

Sample passage:

"Read to me in English," said Papá Grande. Tomás read about tiger eyes shining brightly in the jungle at night. He roared like a huge tiger. Papá, Mamá, and Enrique laughed. They came and sat near him to hear his story. *(p. 17 of unpaged book)*

The Boy Who Was Raised by Librarians by Carla Morris

Because he loves the library, Melvin visits it every day after school. The enthusiastic librarians help him with his many projects and are proud of his accomplishments.

Sample passage:

He wanted to know a little . . . no . . . a lot about everything. He was curious. And the library is a wonderful place to be if a person is curious.

Everything had its place in the library and Melvin liked it that way. His favorite books were always in their places, lined up on the shelves like soldiers. And his favorite people were always in their places behind the reference desk. *(p. 2 of unpaged book)*

The Same Stuff as Stars by Katherine Paterson

While staying with their grandmother on her Vermont farm, Angel and Bernie visit the town's library. Miss Liza sends Angel home with the cookbook she wanted and Bernie with a book about the Stupids.

Sample passage:

Soon Angel could hear Miss Liza's voice reading "One day Stanley Q. Stupid had an idea. This was unusual. "Calling all Stupids!" Stanley shouted.

"Why are they all stupid?" Bernie asked.

"That's their name," said Miss Liza. "Mr. Stanley Q. Stupid, his wife, Mrs. Stupid, Buster Stupid, Petunia Stupid, and their wonderful dog called—Can you guess what they called their dog, Bernie?"

"Stupid!"

"No, they called their dog Kitty."

"Kitty Stupid!" said Bernie, and he laughed right out loud. *(pp. 120–121)*

Delilah D. at the Library by Jeanne Willis

Delilah envisions herself as coming from a land far, far away. When Gigi, their French babysitter takes Delilah and her brother, Smallboy, to the library, she suggests Delilah get help from "that Library Anne." Library Anne's library is very different from Delilah's far, far away library.

Sample passage:

Then [Library Anne] says, "Would you like to borrow a book before you leave?"

Where I come from, we don't borrow books and leave!

We all bring blankets and toys, and a beautiful princess reads to us until we fall asleep. *(pp. 25–26 of unpaged book)*

Age Groups

Group 1: first, second, and third graders, ages six through eight

Group 2: fourth, fifth, and sixth graders, ages nine through eleven

Group 3: seventh and eighth graders, ages twelve through thirteen

Group 4: ninth, tenth, eleventh, and twelfth graders, ages fourteen through seventeen

Timeline: Group 1

Group 1 will meet eleven times over a six-week period. Sessions will typically last about thirty minutes. The group could meet twice a week after school for five weeks or combine sessions and meet for five consecutive Saturdays. Sessions 10 and 11 will need to be at least an hour, if not longer. Session 11 will be on the day before the performance, which will take place in week six.

Session 1
Agenda:
- Have group members introduce themselves.
- Choose a group name.
- Survey books.
- Choose book for Readers Theatre performance.

Make the group feel comfortable. Snacks can help with this. Ask people to introduce themselves and talk a bit about their experiences with libraries. Choosing a group name can encourage bonding.

Show the group these three books: *Delilah D. at the Library, Library Lion, Tomás and the Library Lady*. If possible, bring two copies of each book. Let the children look at the books and choose which one they want to hear first. Read all three books together and then ask the children to choose which one they would like their group to read before an audience in the library. Let them discuss the merits of each book until they can all agree on one. Take a vote, if necessary and appropriate.

Group 1's choice is *Delilah D. at the Library*.

Session 2
Agenda:
- Model Readers Theatre.
- Explore texts converted to scripts.

Now that group members have chosen a book, they are ready to see how they will be using it in the performance. The examples in chapter 6 can be useful at this point. *Wild About Books* would work well with this group. Using a book other than *Delilah D.,* develop a script of your own and ask

colleagues or children to read it to the group with you to model Readers
Theatre. Then show them the original book and explain how the script
uses A, B, C, D to divide up the text and to indicate who will read what.
Explain that this is what they will be doing with *Delilah D. at the Library*.

Session 3

Agenda:
- Type text into computer.

Typing the text into the computer is a group endeavor. Children take turns
reading the text directly from the book while someone (probably you)
types it into the computer. Use the same paragraphing, line breaks, and
punctuation as the book. Don't change font size, even though the text does,
but do use bold print and uppercase just as the text does.

Session 4

Agenda:
- Divide text into parts.

Ask the children to identify how many speakers, or voices, there are in the
book. There will be Delilah, her mother, Gigi, Library Anne, Everybody,
Smallboy, and Mrs. Woolly Hat. Do any speakers say more than the others?
If so, which ones? Who says the most? Could that character's words be
divided between two readers?

If the primary speakers are Delilah 1, Delilah 2, Library Anne, and
Gigi and we have four children in our group, can we double up on parts by
having some readers change their voices and read more than one speaker's
part? Let the children grapple with this question. They will probably come
up with something like

A: Delilah 1
B: Delilah 2
C: Library Anne, Mother, Everyone
D: Gigi, Smallboy, Mrs. Woolly Hat, Everyone

Session 5

Agenda:

- Choose group task responsibility.
- Begin to convert text to script.

Explain that each member needs to take responsibility for a group task. Since there are four people in the group, there will be four tasks:

Director—assigns parts; makes suggestions about how parts are read.

Script keeper—makes copies of each new version of the script and places them in readers' three-ring notebooks.

Stage manager—makes sure the physical environment is ready for performers.

Publicity manager—designs group 1's part of the printed program and troupe publicity.

After group members discuss the tasks, each chooses the one for which he or she will be responsible. There may be some negotiation involved here.

Begin to convert the text to a script by designating readers (A, B, C, or D) for each set of lines. There probably will not be any deletions. The group can all work on this as you make the changes to the text already typed into the computer.

Session 6

Agenda:

- Finish converting text to script.
- Assign parts.

Once the text has been converted to script, the director assigns parts. The script keeper makes copies for all group members and the facilitator.

Session 7

Agenda:

- Begin practicing.

The script keeper brings script copies for everyone. Readers use color-coded markers to highlight their parts on the script. Sit in a circle and read through the text several times. Everyone is welcome to make suggestions regarding interpretation or changes in the script, but the director is in charge of coordinating these. The script keeper notes any changes to the script and runs new copies for the next session.

Session 8
Agenda:
- Continue practicing.

This time readers stand, according to the positions given them by the director, to read the script. Practice turning toward each other during dialogue sequences and using a few appropriate gestures. The publicity manager gathers information about each reader for the printed program.

Session 9
Agenda:
- Continue practicing.

If at all possible, practice in the environment in which the Readers Theatre performance will take place. The stage manager makes sure chairs and stands for holding notebooks are properly arranged. The director helps readers with pacing. The script keeper notes changes and revises scripts if necessary.

Session 10
Agenda:
- Troupe rehearsal 1.

All groups rehearse together in the order of performance. Suggestions are welcome following each segment. If possible, go through the entire program twice.

Session 11
Agenda:
- Troupe rehearsal 2.

Go through the entire program, including entrances and bows. Take comments and then go through one final time.

Timeline: Group 2

Group 2 will meet nine times over a six-week period. Sessions will typically last about forty-five minutes. The group could meet twice a week after school for four weeks or combine sessions and meet for four consecutive Saturdays. Sessions 8 and 9 will probably be longer than an hour. Session 9 will be on the day before the performance, which will take place in week six.

Session 1

Agenda:

- Have group members introduce themselves.
- Choose a group name.
- Survey books.
- Choose book for Readers Theatre performance.

Make the group feel comfortable. Snacks can help with this. Ask people to introduce themselves and talk a bit about their experiences with libraries. Choosing a group name can encourage bonding.

Show the group these three books: *Library Lion, Tomás and the Library Lady,* and *The Boy Who Was Raised by Librarians.* If possible, bring two copies of each book. Let the children look at the books, and then read all three books together. Ask the children to choose which one they would like their group to read before an audience in the library. Let them discuss the merits of each book until they can all agree on one. Take a vote, if necessary and appropriate.

Group 2's choice is *Tomás and the Library Lady.*

Session 2

Agenda:

- Model Readers Theatre.
- Explore texts converted to scripts.
- Type text into computer.

Now that group members have chosen a book, they are ready to see how they will be using it in the performance. The examples in chapter 6 can be useful at this point. *Mike Mulligan and His Steam Shovel* or *Zelda and Ivy* would work well with this group. Using a book other than *Tomás,* develop a script of your own and ask colleagues or children to read it to the group with you as a model Readers Theatre. Then show them the original book and explain how the script uses A, B, C, D to divide up the text and to indicate who will read what. Explain that this is what they will be doing with *Tomás and the Library Lady.*

Typing the text into the computer is a group endeavor. Children can take turns typing into the computer while others take turns reading the text directly from the book. Use the same paragraphing, sentences, punctuation, and italicizing as the book.

Session 3

Agenda:
- Finish typing text into computer.
- Divide text into parts.

Ask the children to identify how many speakers, or voices, there are in the book. There will be Narrator, Tomás, Papá Grande, and Library Lady. Do any speakers say more than the others? If so, which ones? Who says the most? Could that speaker's words be divided between two readers?

There are five children in the group. If the narrator's role is split in two, there will be five major speaking parts—one for each reader:

A: Narrator 1
B: Narrator 2
C: Tomás
D: Papá Grande
E: Library Lady

The readers will be designated as A, B, C, D, E.

Session 4

Agenda:
- Choose group task responsibility.
- Begin to convert text to script.

Explain that each member has to take responsibility for a group task. Since there are five members in the group, the five tasks will be:

Director—assigns parts; makes suggestions about how parts are read.

Script keeper—types in script revisions; makes copies of each new version of script and places them in readers' three-ring notebooks.

Stage manager—makes sure the physical environment is ready for performers.

Publicity manager—designs group 2's part of the printed program and troupe publicity.

Communication coordinator—ensures that everyone knows what is going on in each meeting and that there are no misunderstandings.

After group members discuss the tasks, each chooses the one for which he or she will be responsible. There may be some negotiation involved here.

Begin to convert the text to a script by designating readers (A, B, C, D or E) for each set of lines. There probably will not be many deletions. The group can all work on this as the script keeper modifies the text already typed into the computer.

Session 5

Agenda:
- Finish converting text to script.
- Assign parts.
- Begin practicing.

Once the text has been converted to script, the director assigns parts. The script keeper makes copies for all group members and the facilitator. (This needs to be done while the others take a break.) Readers use color-coded markers to highlight their parts on the script. Sit in a circle and read through the text several times.

Begin practicing. Everyone is welcome to make suggestions regarding interpretation or changes in the script, but the director is in charge of coordinating these. The script keeper notes any changes to the script and runs new copies for the next session.

Session 6

Agenda:

- Continue practicing.

This time readers stand, according to the positions given them by the director, to read the script. Practice turning toward each other during dialogue sequences and using a few appropriate gestures. The publicity manager gathers information about each reader for the printed program.

Session 7

Agenda:

- Continue practicing.

If at all possible, practice in the environment in which the Readers Theatre performance will take place. The stage manager makes sure chairs and stands for holding notebooks are in place. The director helps readers with pacing. The script keeper notes changes and revises scripts if necessary.

Session 8

Agenda:

- Troupe rehearsal 1.

All groups rehearse together in the order of performance. Suggestions are welcome following each segment. If possible, go through the entire program twice.

Session 9

Agenda

- Troupe rehearsal 2.

Go through the entire program, including entrances and bows. Take comments and then go through one final time.

Timeline: Group 3

Group 3 will meet nine times over a six-week period. Sessions will typically last about an hour. The group could meet twice a week after school for four weeks or combine sessions and meet for four consecutive Saturdays. Sessions 8 and 9 may be longer than an hour. Session 9 will be on the day before the performance, which will take place in week six.

Session 1
Agenda:
- Have group members introduce themselves.
- Choose a group name.
- Survey books.
- Choose book for Readers Theatre performance.

Make the group feel comfortable. Snacks can help with this. Ask people to introduce themselves and talk a bit about their experiences with libraries. Choosing a group name can encourage bonding.

Show the group these four books: *Library Lion; The Boy Who Was Raised by Librarians; The Librarian and the Robbers;* and *The Same Stuff as Stars,* chapter 11, "Miss Liza of the Library." If possible, bring two or more copies of each book. Let the group peruse the books and read them together. Then ask them to choose which one they would like their group to read before an audience in the library. Let them discuss the merits of each book until they can all agree on one. Take a vote, if necessary and appropriate.

Group 3's choice is *The Boy Who Was Raised by Librarians.*

Session 2
Agenda:
- Model Readers Theatre.
- Explore texts converted to scripts.
- Type text into computer.

Now that group members have chosen a book, they are ready to see how they will be using it in the performance. The examples in chapter 6 can be useful at this point. *The Penderwicks* or "Shotgun Cheatham's Last Night

Above Ground" would work well with this group. Using a book other than *The Boy Who Was Raised by Librarians,* develop a script of your own and ask colleagues or children to read it to the group with you as a model Readers Theatre. Then show them the original book and explain how the script uses A, B, C, D to divide up the text and to indicate who will read what. Explain that this is what they will be doing with *The Boy Who Was Raised by Librarians.*

Typing the text into the computer is a group endeavor. Members can take turns typing into the computer while the others take turns reading the text directly from the book. Use the same paragraphing, sentences, punctuation, and italicizing as the book.

Session 3

Agenda:
- Finish typing text into computer.
- Divide text into parts.
- Choose group task responsibility.

Ask the group to identify how many speakers, or voices, there are in the book. There will be Narrator, Marge, Betty, Leeola, and Melvin. Do any speakers say more than the others? If so, which ones? Who says the most? Could that speaker's words be divided between two readers?

There are five speakers and there are four people in the group. The readers will be designated as A, B, C, D. The narrator's part is extensive. Can we divide the narrator into four reading parts and double each of these narrators with one of the characters? If this is done, their reading roles will look like this:

A: Narrator 1, Marge
B: Narrator 2, Betty
C: Narrator 3, Leeola
D: Narrator 4, Melvin

Explain that each member needs to take responsibility for a group task. Since there are four members in the group, the four tasks will be:

Director—assigns parts; makes suggestions about how parts are read; ensures that members communicate effectively with one another.

Script keeper—types in script revisions; makes copies of each new version of script and places them in readers' three-ring notebooks.

Stage manager—makes sure the physical environment is ready for performers.

Publicity manager—designs group 3's part of the printed program and troupe publicity.

After group members discuss the tasks, each chooses the one for which he or she will be responsible. There may be some negotiation involved here.

Session 4

Agenda:
- Convert text to script.

Convert the text to a script by designating readers (A, B, C, D) for each set of lines. There probably will not be many deletions besides the speaker signifiers. The group can all work on this as the script keeper modifies the text already typed into the computer.

Session 5

Agenda:
- Finish converting text to script.
- Assign parts.
- Begin practicing.

Once the text has been converted to script, the director assigns parts. The script keeper makes copies for all group members and the facilitator. (This needs to be done while the others take a break.) Readers use color-coded markers to highlight their parts on the script. Sit in a circle and read through the text several times.

Begin practicing. Everyone is welcome to make suggestions regarding interpretation or changes in the script, but the director is in charge of coordinating these. The script keeper notes any changes to the script and runs new copies for the next session.

Session 6
Agenda:
- Continue practicing.

This time readers stand, according to the positions given them by the director, to read the script. Practice turning toward each other during dialogue sequences and using a few appropriate gestures. The publicity manager gathers information about each reader for the printed program.

Session 7
Agenda:
- Continue practicing.

If at all possible, practice in the environment in which the Readers Theatre performance will take place. The stage manager makes sure chairs and stands for holding notebooks are in place. The director helps readers with pacing. The script keeper notes changes and revises scripts if necessary.

Session 8
Agenda:
- Troupe rehearsal 1.

All groups rehearse together in the order of performance. Suggestions are welcome following each segment. If possible, go through the entire program twice.

Session 9
Agenda
- Troupe rehearsal 2.

Go through the entire program, including entrances and bows. Take comments and then go through one final time.

Timeline: Group 4

Group 4 will meet seven times over a six-week period. Sessions will typically last more than an hour. The group could meet once a week after school for five weeks or meet on five consecutive Saturdays. Sessions 6 and 7 will be longer than an hour. Session 7 will be on the day before the performance which will take place in week six.

Session 1

Agenda:

- Have group members introduce themselves.
- Choose a group name.
- Survey books.
- Choose book for Readers Theatre performance.

Make the group feel comfortable. Snacks can help with this. Ask people to introduce themselves and talk a bit about their experiences with libraries. Choosing a group name can encourage bonding.

Show the group these three books: *Library Lion; The Librarian and the Robbers; The Same Stuff as Stars,* chapter 11, "Miss Liza of the Library." If possible, bring two or more copies of each book. In addition, ask the group if they know of other books that feature libraries or librarians they would like the group to consider. Since the group is most likely meeting in the library, they can find copies of these books to add to the suggestion pile. Let the group peruse the books and read them together. Then ask them to choose which one they would like their group to read before an audience in the library. Let them discuss the merits of each book until they can all agree on one. Take a vote, if necessary and appropriate.

Group 4's choice is *The Same Stuff as Stars,* chapter 11, "Miss Liza of the Library."

Session 2

Agenda:

- Model Readers Theatre.
- Explore texts converted to scripts.
- Choose group task responsibility.
- Type text into computer.

Now that group members have chosen a book, they are ready to see how they will be using it in the performance. The examples in chapter 6 can be useful at this point. *Bread and Roses, Too* is ideal, but *Rex Zero and the End of the World* would also work well with this group. Using a book other than *The Same Stuff as Stars,* develop a script of your own and ask colleagues or teens to read it to the group with you to model Readers Theatre. Then show them the original book and explain how the script uses A, B, C, D to divide up the text and to indicate who will read what. Explain that this is what they will be doing with this chapter from *The Same Stuff as Stars.*

Explain that each member needs a group task responsibility. Since there are four people in the group, the four tasks will be:

> **Director**—assigns parts; makes suggestions about how parts are read; ensures that members are communicating effectively with one another.
>
> **Script keeper**—types in script revisions; makes copies of each new version of the script and places them in readers' three-ring notebooks; assembles three script notebooks containing all four scripts for the entire program.
>
> **Stage manager**—makes sure the physical environment is ready for performers; coordinates stage manager efforts for each group and the troupe as a whole.
>
> **Publicity manager**—designs group 4's part of the printed program and troupe publicity; designs and prints program; works with each group's publicity manager to coordinate publicity for troupe.

The script keeper will type the text into the computer exactly as it appears in the book and bring it to the next session on a memory key or laptop.

Session 3

Agenda:
- Divide text into parts.
- Convert text into script.

Ask the group to identify how many speakers, or voices, there are in the chapter. There will be Narrator, Angel, Grandma, Bernie, and Miss Liza. Do any speakers say more than the others? If so, which ones? Who says the most? Could that speaker's words be divided between two readers?

There are five speakers and there are four people in the group. The readers will be designated as A, B, C, D. The narrator's part is extensive. Can we divide the narrator into four reading parts and double each of these narrators with one of the characters? If this is done, their reading roles will look like this:

A: Narrator 1, Angel
B: Narrator 2, Grandma
C: Narrator 3, Bernie
D: Narrator 4, Miss Liza

Working as a team, convert the text to a script by designating readers (A, B, C, D) for each set of lines. Collectively determine what descriptions and speaker signifiers need to be eliminated for the sake of time and pacing. The script keeper modifies the text already typed into the computer, thus creating the group's script.

Session 4
Agenda:
- Assign parts.
- Begin practicing.

The script keeper distributes copies of the script to team members and the facilitator. The director assigns parts. Readers use color-coded markers to highlight their parts on the script.

Begin practicing. Sit in a circle and read through the text several times. Everyone is welcome to make suggestions regarding interpretation or changes in the script, but the director is in charge of coordinating these. The script keeper notes any changes to the script and runs revised copies for the next session.

Session 5

Agenda:

- Continue practicing.

This time readers stand, according to the positions given them by the director, to read the script. Practice turning toward each other during dialogue sequences and using a few appropriate gestures.

If at all possible, practice in the environment in which the Readers Theatre performance will take place. The stage manager makes sure chairs and stands for holding notebooks are in place. The director helps readers with pacing. The script keeper notes changes and revises scripts if necessary.

The publicity manager gathers information about each reader for the printed program.

Session 6

Agenda:

- Troupe rehearsal 1.

All groups rehearse together in the order of performance. Suggestions are welcome following each segment. If possible, go through the entire program twice. The assistant program manager and group 4 stage manager coordinate and troubleshoot.

Session 7

Agenda

- Troupe rehearsal 2.

Go through the entire program, including entrances and bows. Take comments and then go through one final time. The assistant program manager and group 4 stage manager coordinate and troubleshoot.

Performance Day

All four of these timelines converge during National Library Week for the "Libraries in Books" Readers Theatre. The performance is a success, the children and teens have had a rewarding experience, and the community is reminded of the importance of libraries.

Resources

Birdsall, Jeanne. *The Penderwicks: A Summer Tale of Four Sisters, Two Rabbits, and a Very Interesting Boy*. New York: Knopf, 2005.

Burton, Virginia Lee. *Mike Mulligan and His Steam Shovel*. Illus. by author. Boston: Houghton Mifflin, 1939.

Knudsen, Michelle. *Library Lion*. Illus. by Kevin Hawkes. Cambridge, MA: Candlewick, 2006.

Kvasnosky, Laura McGee. *Zelda and Ivy: The Runaways*. Cambridge, MA: Candlewick, 2006.

Mahy, Margaret. *The Great Piratical Rambustification and The Librarian and the Robbers*. Illus. by Quentin Blake. London: Dent, 1978.

Mora, Pat. *Tomás and the Library Lady*. Illus. by Raul Colón. New York: Knopf, 1997. (Published in Spanish as *Tomás y la señora de la biblioteca*.)

Morris, Carla. *The Boy Who Was Raised by Librarians*. Illus. by Brad Sneed. Atlanta, GA: Peachtree, 2007.

Paterson, Katherine. *Bread and Roses, Too*. New York: Clarion, 2006.

———. *The Same Stuff as Stars*. New York: Clarion, 2002.

Peck, Richard. "Shotgun Cheatham's Last Night Above Ground." In *Twelve Shots: Outstanding Short Stories About Guns*, edited by Harry Mazer. New York: Delacorte, 1997.

Sierra, Judy. *Wild About Books*. Illus. by Marc Brown. New York: Knopf, 2004.

Willis, Jeanne. *Delilah D. at the Library*. Illus. by Rosie Reeve. New York: Clarion, 2007. (Originally published in Great Britain by Puffin, 2006.)

Wynne-Jones, Tim. *Rex Zero and the End of the World*. New York: Melanie Kroupa/ Farrar Straus Giroux, 2007. (Originally published in Canada by Groundwood, 2006.)

Books to Consider

One Hundred Titles That Would Make Good Readers Theatre

THERE ARE, OF COURSE, HUNDREDS AND HUNDREDS OF BOOKS THAT would make good Readers Theatre. The titles listed here represent various formats and genres that offer potentially excellent material for children and teens interested in creating Readers Theatre experiences. The list consists of books I have seen successfully performed by one group or another, books I have used in various teaching situations, books for which I have written educator's guides, books by authors with whom I have worked closely, books that were favorites of my own children, books that I have considered when a member of one book award committee or another, books that I loved as a child, books that I discovered as an adult, books that I have had for many years, and books that I have recently acquired.

I did not select these books with any social or political issues in mind. My overarching consideration was that each book be an example of high quality literature that contains at least one section that could be converted into an effective Readers Theatre script and subsequent performance. I also did not take into account whether or not the book is still in print because out-of-print books can, thankfully, still be found in libraries. When reviewing books for inclusion here, I envisioned how each one could be used by children or teens in a Readers Theatre production. This list is neither exclusive nor comprehensive. Ideally, after becoming familiar with the types of books that work well, children and teens, teachers and librarians, parents and friends will develop their own lists based on their personal Readers Theatre expertise.

The category in which a book is included is usually based on the age level of the audience rather than the ages of the Readers Theatre troupe members and takes into account that the listeners will not have the visual clues provided by picture books. Listeners in a suggested age group may or may not be able to read the books themselves, but they can appreciate hearing age-appropriate literature read by practiced performers. Performing for a younger audience, as indicated in the opening scenario in chapter 1, can be an ideal situation. Generally speaking, books for very young audiences would be for listeners from three to five years of age, or preschool through kindergarten. Books for young audiences would be for listeners from six to seven years of age, or grades one through two. Books for intermediate-level audiences would be for listeners from seven to ten years of age, or grades three through five. Books for middle-level audiences would be for listeners from ten to twelve years of age, or grades six through seven. Books for young adult audiences would be most appropriate for teen listeners, or eighth grade and up. These are general guidelines. Individual librarians or teachers would know best which books would be appropriate for the young people with whom they work. And, of course, older listeners can readily enjoy well-done presentations of books appropriate for audiences other than themselves. As experienced educators know, a good book can be appreciated by a variety of audiences.

Books for Very Young Audiences

Bang, Molly. *When Sophie Gets Angry—Really, Really Angry.* . . .
Illus. by author. New York: Blue Sky/Scholastic, 1999.
When Sophie gets angry she kicks, screams, runs, climbs trees, cries, and communes with nature. Then she returns to the restored harmony of home. The overt drama of the story, the augmenting sound effects, and the quiet

ending make this an excellent vehicle for expressive reading. It would be an ideal choice for older children to read to younger children via Readers Theatre.

Becker, John. *Seven Little Rabbits.*
Illus. by Barbara Cooney. New York: Walker, 1973.
As seven little rabbits take a walk down the road to call on their "old friend toad," they one by one tire and fall asleep in a mole's hill. Rhythmic repetition of words, phrases, and events make this circular tale delightfully well suited for Readers Theatre.

Brown, Margaret Wise. *The Runaway Bunny.*
Illus. by Clement Hurd. New York: HarperCollins, 1972. (Originally published in 1942.)
Each time the little bunny thinks of a way to run away from his mother, the mother bunny counters with how she will come after him. The loving reassurance offered by the story is reinforced by the repeated phrasing of the if-then narrative structure. This story would work wonderfully with two main readers for the bunnies and a third minor reader taking the opening and closing narrative parts.

Burton, Virginia Lee. *Mike Mulligan and His Steam Shovel.*
Illus. by author. Boston: Houghton Mifflin, 1939.
In an effort to show what a good digging team he and his steam shovel, Mary Anne, are, Mike Mulligan accepts a challenge to dig the cellar for the new town hall in just one day. Big machines, loyal friends, community spirit, and the drama of a challenge make this a book that continues to appeal to generations of children. See chapter 6 for an example of how this book can be used as Readers Theatre.

Cowley, Joy. *Mrs. Wishy-Washy.*
Illus. by Elizabeth Fuller. Originally published in Auckland, New Zealand: Short-land, 1980. (Other Mrs. Wishy-Washy books published in the US by Philomel.)
Mrs. Wishy-Washy cleans up a cow, a pig, and a duck, only to have them joyfully return to the mud. With parts for four characters, this story is already a Readers Theatre script—no alterations required! As with *A Kitten Tale,* I suggest the speaker signifiers remain for the sake of narrative flow.

While I am partial to the original, any of the Mrs. Wishy-Washy books would make fine Readers Theatre.

Henkes, Kevin. *Julius, The Baby of the World.*
Illus. by author. New York: Greenwillow, 1990.
Lilly wants her baby brother to go away, but her parents say he is here to stay. Lilly's pure drama makes this book an excellent choice for Readers Theatre, and its delightful humor guarantees it will be a hit. Reading parts divide naturally with each sentence break, and there is ample opportunity for vocal expression.

Henkes, Kevin. *Lilly's Purple Plastic Purse.*
Illus. by author. New York: Greenwillow, 1996.
Lilly loves her teacher, Mr. Slinger, but she becomes angry with him when he confiscates her purple plastic purse. Lilly's exuberance would be lots of fun to portray with Readers Theatre. As with *Julius, the Baby of the World,* each line could be read by a different reader, making it easy to divide the story into parts.

Hoban, Russell. *A Bargain for Frances.*
Illus. by Lillian Hoban. New York: HarperCollins, 1970.
Thelma frequently gets the better of Frances, but this time Frances comes out on top with the tea set she wants while maintaining her friendship with Thelma. The book's ample, lively dialogue could easily be divided among four readers. One could be Frances; one could be both Frances' mother and her younger sister Gloria; one could be Thelma; and one could be the narrator. All the speaker signifiers could be eliminated and an occasional name inserted to indicate to whom the character is speaking. All four readers could join together to help Frances sing her songs. Loved by children for over forty years, the Frances books are excellent candidates for Readers Theatre.

Hoberman, Mary Ann. *You Read to Me, I'll Read to You:*
Very Short Stories to Read Together.
Illus. by Michael Emberley. New York: Little, Brown, 2001.
These very short but highly appealing stories are already divided into parts for two readers. The introduction explains that the purple words on the

left are read by one reader, the red words on the right are read by another reader, and the blue words in the middle are read together. A Readers Theatre group of six readers could take turns reading the various stories in pairs.

Lobel, Arnold. *Frog and Toad Are Friends.*
Illus. by author. New York: Harper and Row, 1970.
The abiding friendship between Frog and Toad makes their gently humorous adventures an excellent Readers Theatre offering. Readers can select favorites from the five stories or include them all. Selections will generally require one or more narrators to augment the dialogue of Frog and Toad. In preparation for the performance, readers can explore personality differences between Frog and Toad and their resulting speech patterns. This close reading will enable readers to differentiate between Frog and Toad by the way they read their lines, making it possible to eliminate many of the speaker signifiers in the narrative. For these same reasons, *Frog and Toad All Year* (Harper, 1975) would also be a worthy Readers Theatre choice.

Lobel, Arnold. *Mouse Tales.*
Illus. by author. New York: Harper and Row, 1972.
Seven tales for seven mice told by their father at bedtime make *Mouse Tales* an endearing story collection. With its numerous rodent characters, as well as a wishing well and the four winds, this book could easily involve a large group of children, each taking a small reading part in one of the seven stories. A narrator announcing the various titles would lend a sense of ceremony to the reading.

McCloskey, Robert. *Make Way for Ducklings.*
New York: Viking, 1941.
A picture book classic, this engaging story of a duck family assisted by the friendly Boston police force would lend itself well to a Readers Theatre. I would suggest four narrators: one general, one associated with Mr. Mallard, one with Mrs. Mallard, one with the policemen. All four could join together for the duckling quacks. The speaker signifiers should remain in the script, for the most part, as they are generally coupled with actions necessary for advancing the story. If it seems performing the entire book

may exceed young listeners' attention spans, consider suggesting an intermission midway through the story.

Rohmann, Eric. *A Kitten Tale.*

Illus. by author. New York: Knopf, 2008.
Four kittens that have never seen snow share their fears and wonder at
this phenomenon. The elegant simplicity of the language and the exacting
rhythm of the text make repeated readings delightful for both reader and
listener. The opportunity to add a bit of dialogue to the script explaining
the pictorial depiction of three kittens hiding when the snow begins to fall
offers an appropriate challenge to young Readers Theatre performers. (See
chapter 6.)

Sendak, Maurice. *Chicken Soup with Rice: A Book of Months.*

New York: HarperCollins, 1962.
Take four readers, assign each reader to every fourth month of the year,
have all four readers form a chorus to read the various refrains for each
month, and voilá, you have a foolproof recipe for superb *Chicken Soup with
Rice* Readers Theatre. Then sit back and enjoy the delicious performance!

Slobodkina, Esphyr. *Caps for Sale: A Tale of a Peddler, Some Monkeys and Their Monkey Business.*

*Illus. by author. New York: HarperCollins, 1968. (First published in New York by
William R. Scott in 1940.)*
A favorite with preschoolers for over seventy years, this classic story of the
monkeys who steal the peddler's caps and imitate his every move is ideal
for Readers Theatre. The listings of kinds of hats piled atop the peddler's
head, the repeated phrases, the imitated speech ("Tsz, tsz, tsz") would all
make for a memorable performance. The text would need no altering, just
division of parts among readers.

Yolen, Jane. *Owl Moon.*

Illus. by John Schoenherr. New York: Philomel, 1987.
This quiet story of a child and her father going owling in the middle of a
winter night invites reading in hushed voices. The text is already a Readers
Theatre script; parts need only to be assigned. Because it is told from the
girl's point of view, her voice can be divided among several readers. The

father would be another reader, with readers doubling up for the brothers and the owl. The lyrical flow of the words and the awesomeness of the situation make this book a superb Readers Theatre selection.

Books for Young Audiences

Almond, David. *Kate, the Cat and the Moon.*
Illus by Stephen Lambert. New York: Doubleday, 2005. (Originally published in Great Britain by Hodder, 2004.)
Transformed into a cat, Kate accompanies a fellow feline on a moonlight adventure. The language, rhythm, repeated phrases, and parallel constructions make this an excellent candidate for Readers Theatre. It is easy to envision the book divided into parts for Kate, the cat, and the moon, along with their associated narrators, and members of her family. Several opportunities for characters to speak in unison add to the book's already strong potential.

Fine, Anne. *Jamie and Angus Together.*
Illus. by Penny Dale. Cambridge, MA: Candlewick, 2007. (Originally published in Great Britain by Walker, 2007.)
These linguistically sophisticated stories about Jamie, an older preschooler, and his beloved stuffed animal, a Highland bull, can be readily enjoyed by children who probably are past preschool themselves but may relish a nostalgic look at outgrown behaviors. The humorous story "A Nice Long Walk in the Country Without Any Fussing" would work well as a Readers Theatre script because it has four speakers and a narrator. The antics of Uncle Edward would be fun for both performers and audience. Other stories in *Jamie and Angus Together* as well as in *The Jamie and Angus Stories* (Candlewick, 2002) would also make fine choices.

Fleming, Candace. *Boxes for Katje.*
Illus. by Stacey Dressen-McQueen. New York: Melanie Kroupa/Farrar Straus Giroux, 2003.
When the war ends, American children send boxes of hard-to-find items to children of Holland. Katje receives several boxes and shares their contents with the residents of her Dutch town of Olst. The lively writing and many

speaking parts will convert readily into an excellent script. The German phrases spoken by Katje's neighbors and the letters exchanged by Katje and Rosie will add special touches to the performance.

Hobbs, Will. *Beardream.*
Illus. by Jill Kastner. New York: Atheneum, 1997.
Even though the illustrations add another dimension to this picture book, the text aptly tells the story of the first Ute Bear Dance and could easily be adapted for Readers Theatre. To do this, I would eliminate the "said"s but provide the instructions accompanying them in italics for the readers' benefit. Actions attached to dialogue can be transposed into sentences to be read by one of the multiple narrators. Transcribing this text into a script presents manageable challenges that require clear understanding of the narrative as well as the author's style.

Howe, James. *Houndsley and Catina and the Birthday Surprise.*
Illus. by Marie-Louise Gay. Cambridge, MA: Candlewick, 2006.
The empathic friendship shared by this cat and dog evolves into a mutual birthday, complete with two surprise parties. The highly satisfying ending would make this an appealing Readers Theatre presentation. Not much more than eliminating the speaker signifiers and assigning parts would need to be done to convert the narrative into a script.

Knudsen, Michelle. *Library Lion.*
Illus. by Kevin Hawkes. Cambridge, MA: Candlewick, 2006.
There are no rules about lions in the library, or lions at story hour, but there are rules about making noise. So a nice, quiet lion can come to story hour. He can also assist with library chores, help the small children, and aid an injured librarian. But if he roars, he has to go. This quietly humorous picture book would be an excellent choice for a Readers Theatre program focusing on libraries, or rules, or helpful friends. The text contains ample dialogue for a lively reading performance.

Kvasnosky, Laura McGee. *Zelda and Ivy: The Runaways.*
Cambridge, MA: Candlewick, 2006.
This is a chapter book with three self-contained stories featuring the Fox sisters, so a Readers Theatre performance could consist of three differ-

ent readings with three different casts. Alternatively, readers may want to choose chapter stories from the various Zelda and Ivy books and combine them into a performance designed around their favorites. In any case, the situations in which Zelda and Ivy find themselves provide engaging scenarios for young listeners. (See chapter 6.)

Livingston, Myra Cohn. *Birthday Poems.*
Illus. by Margot Tomes. New York: Holiday House, 1989.
These poems are all about birthdays. I particularly like the one titled "Presents" because it lists all the presents the child received and ends with personalized stationery to write thank-you notes to friends. This list and others found in various poems provide opportunities for quick pacing among Readers Theatre participants, making for energetic presentations. Performing accessible poetry such as "Presents" in a Readers Theatre setting can ease young patrons into the pleasure of poetry

Mahy, Margaret. *Bubble Trouble.*
Illus. by Polly Dunbar. New York: Clarion, 2009. (First published in the United Kingdom by Frances Lincoln, 2008.)
Told in impeccable rhyming couplets, this book about a baby in a bubble begs to be read in Readers Theatre. Listeners of all ages will delight to Mahy's compelling rhythm, intricate rhymes, alluring alliteration, and zany vocabulary. Readers will have great fun tripping over their tongues while performing this perfect Readers Theatre selection. (See chapter 6.)

Mora, Pat. *Tomás and the Library Lady.*
Illus. by Raul Colón. New York: Knopf, 1997. (Published in Spanish as Tomás y la señora de la biblioteca.)
Tomás loves to hear stories. At his grandfather's suggestion, he visits the public library, where the kind librarian gives him water for his thirst and books for his imagination. Based on the life of Tomás Rivera, a migrant worker who grew up to be the chancellor of the University of California at Riverside, this picture book would work well in Readers Theatre presentations about libraries, migrant workers, grandfathers, and bibliophiles. The Spanish words in the English version and the English words in the Spanish version would make a linguistically distinctive performance.

Morales, Yuyi. *Just in Case: A Trickster Tale and Spanish Alphabet Book.*
Illus. by author. New York: Roaring Brook, 2008.
This bilingual picture book—with its playfully haunting story, its mix of English and Spanish, and Zelmiro's repeated phrases urging Señor Calavera to look for one more present for Grandma Beetle "[j]ust in case"—makes for delightfully unusual Readers Theatre. Four readers would be perfect here: one associated with Señor Calavera, the skeleton; one associated with Zelmiro the Ghost; one to speak the Spanish words given in alphabetical order; and one to provide each word's English definition and additional commentary.

Morris, Carla. *The Boy Who Was Raised by Librarians.*
Illus. by Brad Sneed. Atlanta, GA: Peachtree, 2007.
The friendly, resourceful librarians of Livingston Public Library respond to Melvin's insatiable curiosity with books, Internet links, and unwavering enthusiasm. Multiple narrators doubling up for the parts of the three librarians and Melvin would provide for an entertaining, enlightening Readers Theatre performance. This picture book is an excellent selection for a program focusing on the topic of libraries.

Park, Linda Sue. *The Firekeeper's Son.*
Illus. by Julie Downing. New York: Clarion, 2004.
Set in Korea during the early 1800s, this is the story of Sang-hee, the son of the man who lights the first in a chain of fires signaling to the king that no enemies come from the sea. Although tempted not to light the fire and thereby summon the king's soldiers, Sang-hee lights the fire to signal that all is well in the land and settles for visions of soldiers he sees in the flames. The rhythm and pacing of the text make this picture book a worthy Readers Theatre candidate.

Partridge, Elizabeth. *Whistling.*
Illus. by Anna Grossnickle. New York: Greenwillow, 2003.
A young boy and his father camp out all night and then whistle up the sun. This quiet, unusual father-son story would make an interesting Readers Theatre presentation for four readers—father, son, and two narrators. Opportunities for whispering and whistling would add auditory variety to the performance.

Paterson, Katherine. *Marvin One Too Many.*
Illus. by Jane Clark Brown. New York: HarperCollins, 2001.
Because it is about learning to read, this Marvin book would work well for children involved in the process. The school and family situations may strike familiar chords. The story's warmth and humor provide appeal for audiences of all ages. (See chapter 6.)

Rohmann, Eric. *Pumpkinhead.*
New York: Knopf, 2003.
This short adventurous tale about Otho, who was born with a pumpkin for a head, could be easily converted into an enjoyable Readers Theatre script. The text would not need to be altered at all, just divided into parts. The lines for the bat and fisherman would be particularly fun to read. The bat speaks in rhyme, and the fisherman lists the twenty-eight types of fish he has previously caught; they all end in *fish,* including the new pumpkinfish. Along with his adventures, Pumpkinhead basks in the unconditional love and eternal optimism of caring parents.

Robb, Laura, compiler. *Snuffles and Snouts.*
Illus. by Steven Kellogg. New York: Dial, 1995.
Selected from contemporary, classic, and traditional sources, all the poems in this collection have to do with pigs, an animal popular with many children. When dialogue does not determine readers' parts, alternating readers from verse to verse can create highly enjoyable Readers Theatre with this and other poetry collections as well.

Sierra, Judy. *Wild About Books.*
Illus. by Marc Brown. New York: Knopf, 2004.
This book is perfect for Readers Theatre, both in content and form. It's the story of librarian Molly McGrew, who mistakenly drives her bookmobile into the zoo and turns the animals into readers. Written in couplets, with rhythm and rhyme that fall trippingly from the tongue, this book is a joy to read and hear. See chapter 6 for one way the lines can be divided among readers.

Sullivan, Sarah. *Once Upon a Baby Brother.*
Illus. by Tricia Tusa. New York: Farrar Straus Giroux, 2010.
Beautifully written with both humor and pathos, this story of a second-grade writer and her pesky baby brother would be lots of fun to perform as Readers Theatre. The words tell most of the story, but the page where the illustrations contradict the text would provide an appropriate challenge for readers to add a few lines of text as they convert the book into a script.

Willis, Jeanne. *Delilah D. at the Library.*
Illus. by Rosie Reeve. New York: Clarion, 2007. (Originally published in Great Britain by Puffin, 2006.)
Delilah loves books, the library, and even the sensible Library Anne. However, Delilah has her own views on how a library should be operated. This delightful romp with an exuberant young patron would be a wonderfully humorous addition to a themed presentation of books about libraries. Visual clues provided by the typography would vividly enhance a Readers Theatre performance. This book is really too good to miss.

Woodson, Jacqueline. *The Other Side.*
Illus. by E. B. Lewis. New York: Putnam, 2001.
This gentle story of children overcoming racial boundaries holds strong potential for a Readers Theatre selection. When Jacqueline Woodson prepared its script for the 2010 ALA Readers Theatre in Washington, D.C., she divided the role of the narrator into parts for several readers, with narrators doubling as Sandra, Annie, Clover, and Clover's mama. This book would work well in a themed Readers Theatre presentation on friendship.

Wynne-Jones, Tim. *Zoom.*
Illus. by Eric Beddows. Toronto: Groundwood, 2009.
Although I would probably begin with the first tale, "Zoom at Sea," all three stories about Zoom the cat would aptly lend themselves to a Readers Theatre performance. Tim Wynne-Jones's verbal descriptions of the action and scenery in the stories paint such vivid images that the illustrations, although stunning, are not really necessary. Readers Theatre listeners will readily succumb to the lulling rhythm and flow of the words as they visualize Zoom's magical travels and eagerly accompany him on his journeys.

Books for Intermediate-Level Audiences

Almond, David. *The Boy Who Climbed into the Moon.*
Illus. by Polly Dunbar. Somerville, MA: Candlewick, 2010. (Originally published in England by Walker, 2010.)
David Almond's superb sense of rhythm and pacing along with quirky characters, whimsical dialogue, and witty word play make this surreal tale a delightful selection for Readers Theatre. With so many high potential scenes to choose from, it would be hard to go wrong. In addition to the chapter Almond selected for the 2010 IBBY Readers Theatre in Santiago de Compostela (see chapter 6), the elevator scene, in which Tom, the lift inspector, conducts a ridiculous survey of elevator riders as they travel up to the twenty-ninth floor while a very tall ladder, the ladder that will enable Paul to climb into the moon, is being passed hand to hand up the outside of the building, would be great Readers Theatre fun. The scene with Paul actually inside the moon would also work well. The book's British flavor adds to its appeal.

Atinuke. *Anna Hibiscus.*
Illus. by Lauren Tobia. San Diego, CA: Kane Miller, 2010. (Originally published in England by Walker, 2007.)
"Anna Hibiscus lives in Africa. Amazing Africa." So begins each of the stories in this appealing collection of stories. The first story, "Anna Hibiscus on Holiday," would be a wonderful place to begin because it introduces readers to Anna's large extended family and their African customs. Minor deletions from the text and multiple narrators doubling as family members are all that would be needed to convert Anna's stories to lively Readers Theatre. Occasional bits of dialect provide a bonus for performers and their audience.

Birdsall, Jeanne. *The Penderwicks: A Summer Tale of Four Sisters, Two Rabbits, and a Very Interesting Boy.*
New York: Knopf, 2005.
Likeable characters, exciting adventures, loyal family and friends all converge to make *The Penderwicks* perfect for Readers Theatre performances. (See chapter 6.) The other books in this series, *The Penderwicks on Gardam*

Street (Knopf, 2008) and *The Penderwicks at Point Mouette* (Knopf, 2011), also offer excellent Readers Theatre fare. Because each book introduces new characters, it might be fun to have a cross-series Readers Theatre called "Introducing the Penderwick Family and Friends" that highlights each character as he or she enters the Penderwick world.

Cleary, Beverly. *Beezus and Ramona.*
Illus. by Louis Darling. New York: William Morrow, 1955.
It is difficult to know which Ramona book to list here because all would provide marvelous Readers Theatre experiences, but since *Beezus and Ramona* sets the stage for the series, it is a logical starting point. The scene in which Ramona, pretending to be Gretel pushing the witch into the oven, puts her rubber doll in Beezus's birthday cake while it bakes, is one of many hilarious episodes in life with Ramona. Whole Readers Theatre programs drawing from all eight Ramona books (the other seven are: *Ramona the Pest,* Morrow, 1968; *Ramona the Brave,* Morrow, 1975; *Ramona and Her Father,* Morrow, 1977; *Ramona and Her Mother,* Morrow, 1979; *Ramona Quimby, Age 8,* Morrow, 1981; *Ramona Forever,* Morrow, 1984; *Ramona's World,* Morrow, 1999) would have cross-generational appeal. These insightful children's classics have been loved by readers of all ages for nearly sixty years.

Delacre, Lulu. *Salsa Stories.*
Illus. by author. New York: Scholastic, 2000.
When a friend gives Carmen Teresa a blank book for a New Year's gift, friends and family at the holiday dinner tell her stories they think should be recorded in the book. The stories, which include many Spanish words and phrases, are about their childhood holiday experiences in the various Latin American countries in which they grew up. Instead, Carmen Teresa chooses to fill her book with recipes for the delicious Latin American food the others mention in their stories. The stories, any of which could be used in and of themselves, would make informative, entertaining Readers Theatre scripts. The recipes could be used to prepare enticing intermission refreshments.

DiCamillo, Kate. *Because of Winn-Dixie.*
Cambridge, MA: Candlewick, 2000.
India Opal Buloni's engaging voice and her compelling story of stray dog Winn-Dixie combine to create a satisfying narrative that will work well as

Readers Theatre. The chapter in which Opal takes Winn-Dixie home to her father, the preacher, would be an excellent choice to read because it introduces several major characters and shows the positive effect Winn-Dixie has on people. On the other hand, the fast-paced chapter in which Winn-Dixie goes berserk, showing the dog's deep-seated fear of thunderstorms, would be exciting to read. Because there is so much first-person narration, I suggest using two narrators.

Funke, Cornelia. *Igraine the Brave.*
Illus. by author. Trans. by Anthea Bell. New York: Chicken House/Scholastic, 2007. (Originally published in Germany by Cecilie Dressler, 1998.)
Adventures abound in this world of knights, besieged castles, powerful magicians, singing magic books, and magic gone wrong. Exciting scenes include Brave Igraine's quest for hairs from a red-headed giant, Igraine and the Sorrowful Knight entering the castle through the mouth of an enchanted stone lion (see chapter 6), and the one-on-one combat between the Sorrowful Knight (assisted by his squire, Igraine) and Rowan the Heartless. All in all, this book holds great potential for captivating Readers Theatre.

Gaiman, Neil. *Coraline.*
Illus. by Dave McKean. New York: HarperCollins, 2002. (Originally published in Great Britain by Bloomsbury, 2002.)
While exploring her new flat, Coraline discoverers another mother who wants Coraline to stay with her forever. Brave and resourceful, Coraline saves herself, rescues her parents and three lost souls, and rids the house of the evil entity posing as her "other mother." This eerie tale of the supernatural has great potential to produce spine-tingling Readers Theatre. The scenes where Coraline explores the flat on the other side of the magic door and where the other mother puts her in a closet with three past victims have ample dialogue and vivid descriptions, making them outstanding choices for delightfully scary scripts.

Gaiman, Neil. *Odd and the Frost Giants.*
Illus. by Brett Helquist. New York: Harper, 2009. (Originally published in Great Britain by Bloomsbury, 2008.)
Despite his shattered leg, a Viking boy by the name of Odd travels to Asgard, the city of the gods, with three members of the Norse astir—Thor, Odin, and Loki—who have been transformed into animals by a Frost Giant. Inspired by Norse mythology, this tale is highly entertaining and deeply

satisfying. The chapter called "The Night Conversation," in which Odd discovers the true identity of his companions, has some priceless dialogue that would make hilarious Readers Theatre.

Lin, Grace. *Where the Mountain Meets the Moon.*
Illus. by author. New York: Little, Brown, 2009.
In this fantasy inspired by Chinese folktales, Minli travels to the Never-Ending Mountain to ask the Old Man in the Moon an important question. She meets a dragon who accompanies her on her quest. The threads from the stories within the story cleverly entwine to weave an intriguing tale with a satisfying ending. The chapter in which Minli and the dragon outfox the greedy monkeys would be fun to do as Readers Theatre. It would make an excellent companion to *Caps for Sale* and *Shiva's Fire* in a presentation featuring monkey business in children's books.

Lindgren, Astrid. *Pippi Longstocking.*
Illus. by Louis S. Glanzman. New York: Viking, 1950. (Originally published in Sweden.)
The antics of the irrepressible Pippi Longstocking, a popular literary character for over sixty years, would make lively Readers Theatre. Tales of Pippi playing tag with policemen, performing in a circus, and saving children from a burning building could all be dramatic presentations, but "Pippi Goes to School" is bound to have audiences laughing out loud. Other books from the series, such as *Pippi Goes on Board* (Viking, 1957) and *Pippi of the South Seas* (Viking, 1959), also offer abundant opportunities for exuberant performances.

Lowry, Lois. *Bless This Mouse.*
Illus. by Eric Rohmann. New York: Houghton Mifflin, 2011.
A purely delightful tale of resourcefulness and bravery, this story of church mice holds myriad possibilities for Readers Theatre. The opening chapter would work well as an introduction to the vigilant life required of the mice living around people. Scenes involving Mouse Mistress Hildegard giving instructions to her clan, her humorous conversations with the scholarly Ignatius, and her amazing rescue of her obnoxious rival Lucretia would also make lively performances. Since there are few scenes with more than two characters conversing, it might be most effective to designate several

narrators when converting the text to a script. Otherwise, the text would need little revision besides eliminating the speaker identifiers.

Machado, Ana Maria. *From Another World.*
Illus. by Lúcia Brandão. Trans. by Luisa Baeta. Toronto: Groundwood, 2005.
(Originally published in Brazil by Editora Ática, 2002.)
Set in contemporary Brazil, this friendly ghost story provides historical insight into the plight of nineteenth-century slaves on Brazilian coffee plantations. By disclosing the tragic events that led to her death and procuring a promise that they will be written down to share with others so such cruelties will never happen again, Rosario is now able to rest in peace. (See chapter 6.)

Mahy, Margaret. *The Great Piratical Rumbustification* **and** *The Librarian and the Robbers.*
Illus. by Quentin Blake. London: Dent, 1978.
Although both stories in this duo are highly entertaining, "The Librarian and the Robbers" is priceless Readers Theatre material. The book's outrageous premise, the conversion of a band of rambunctious robbers into respectable, albeit unusual, librarians, coupled with Margaret Mahy's impeccable pacing, diction, and sense of humor, make this a literary treasure—with homage to the power of books to joyfully improve lives. Converting the text to a script requires not much more than eliminating the speaker identifiers. Copies of this story may be hard to find, but they are definitely worth the search.

Park, Linda Sue. *Tap Dancing on the Roof: Sijo (Poems).*
Illus. by Istvan Banyai. New York: Clarion, 2007.
This delightful collection of *sijo*, a Korean form of poetry, takes us through the seasons with three-line and six-line poems. Humor, clever insights, and carefully chosen language make Linda Sue Park's *sijo* highly enjoyable possibilities for Readers Theatre. (See chapter 6.)

Peck, Richard. *Secrets at Sea.*
Illus. by Kelly Murphy. New York: Dial, 2011.
Adventures abound as Helena and her mouse siblings surreptitiously take to the sea with their family, the Upstairs Cranstons. Master storyteller

Richard Peck's keen ear for language, acute sense of timing, graceful prose, dry wit, and delightful details make this entertaining and deeply satisfying tale a winning choice for Readers Theatre. Transposing any section into a script will need little more than eliminating speaker signifiers. Two narrators, one general and one associated with Helen, would work well.

Ryan, Pam Muñoz. *The Dreamer.*
Illus. by Peter Sís. New York: Scholastic, 2010.
Neftalí's harsh father abhors the fact that his son is a dreamer, a collector, and a word lover. In fluid lyrical prose, Pam Muñoz Ryan offers this fictional account of poet Pablo Neruda's life from childhood to his beginning literary career, when he assumes his pseudonym to avoid embarrassing his family by being a poet with liberal politics. The chapter in which the librarian at the Chilean beach town where the family summers supplies Neftalí with books and a hideout in which to read them would make an impressive Readers Theatre presentation.

White, E. B. *Charlotte's Web.*
Illus. by Garth Williams. New York: Harper and Row, 1952.
Written in elegant prose with flawless rhythm and exquisite word choice, E. B. White's masterpiece is an enduring story of friendship and the web of life. Although any part of this classic could easily convert to a superb Readers Theatre script, the chapters in which Charlotte and Wilbur meet, "Loneliness" and "Charlotte," would make for a triumphant performance. White's other two celebrated books, *Stuart Little* (Harper and Row, 1945) and *Trumpet of the Swan* (Harper and Row, 1970), would also make excellent Readers Theatre choices.

Woodson, Jacqueline. *Show Way.*
Illus. by Hudson Talbott. New York: Putnam, 2005.
Jacqueline Woodson's lyrical text chronicles the multifaceted legacy of Show Way quilts that directed enslaved people along the Underground Railroad. The beauty of the language, the natural ebb and flow of the words, and the recurring phrases and refrains combine to stitch together the lineage of a child and the history of a people. Multiple narrators would make this story an effective Readers Theatre piece.

Middle-Level Books

Anderson, M. T. *The Game of Sunken Places.*
New York: Scholastic, 2004.
The grace and intellect with which Tobin Anderson writes would make it easy to convert this suspenseful and humorous novel into an appealing Readers Theatre script. A performance of the second chapter could entice audience members to read the complete book and even the entire Norumbegan Quartet. In the spirit of not spoiling the fun of reading this exciting mystery adventure, it might be best to perform other scenes only for audiences who have read the book. However, if the audience is already familiar with the book, it would be great fun to read some of the key scenes to recap the book's intriguing premise and intricate plot.

Avi. *"Who Was That Masked Man, Anyway?"*
New York: Orchard, 1992.
Except for excerpts from old radio plays, this entire novel is written in dialogue without any speaker signifiers, making it practically a Readers Theatre script already. The scenes in which Franklin and Mario pretend they are hero and sidekick would make lively duet performances, but there are also scenes that involve three or more characters—such as when the boys are caught in the room of the man who boards with Franklin's family. This novel might work well in a themed performance along with others set in the United States during World War II.

Bredsdorff, Bodil. *Tink.*
Trans. by Elisabeth Kellick Dyssegaard. New York: Farrar Straus Giroux, 2011. (Originally published in Denmark by Høst and Son, 1994.)
The third book in The Children of Crow Cove series, *Tink* would make particularly engaging Readers Theatre. The friendship between Tink, a sensitive orphan boy, and Burd, an abusive drunkard, highlights the complexity of human relationships. The chapter in which Burd saves Tink's life would make a poignant presentation as would the one in which Tink learns to whittle small farm animals. *The Crow Girl* (Farrar Straus Giroux, 2004) and *Eidi* (Farrar Straus Giroux, 2009) would also make excellent Readers Theatre, but they are probably better suited for a younger audience.

Bryan, Ashley, reteller. *African Tales, Uh-Huh.*
Illus. by author. New York: Atheneum, 1998.
The rhythm of the language in these African folktales makes them natural candidates for exciting Readers Theatre performances. For example, "The Foolish Boy," an Ananse trickster tale about a foolish boy who becomes wise, has songs and refrains that could be sung or recited in unison as well as lots of onomatopoeia that would be fun to read aloud. Several of the tales use similar storytelling techniques. Once children have found the stories that interest them most, converting them to scripts will merely be a matter of assigning parts, occasionally omitting the speaker identifiers, and having fun with the language.

Cheng, Andrea. *Where the Steps Were.*
Honesdale, PA: Wordsong, 2008.
This novel in verse is told from the perspectives of five third graders whose school will be demolished at the end of the year. Although it may seem a natural literary format for Readers Theatre, a novel in verse told from multiple perspectives holds particular challenges. This novel has multiple speakers, each recounting his or her own experiences, with little interaction among the characters. Their stories intertwine, but there is not a self-contained section that could be performed independently of the complete book.

For this reason, I suggest the entire book be performed in Readers Theatre circles composed of six readers, five taking the parts of the students and one taking the role of the teacher who is frequently quoted in the students' poems. The Readers Theatre circles would hold a series of informal readings without an audience other than themselves. This idea is inspired by a real-life situation in which students from the school featured in the book took the multiple copies of the book that were placed in the literature corner and decided to "play *Steps,*"as they called it. They didn't have to create a script for their Readers Theatre, but my suggestion of adding a sixth voice for the teacher would require the group to identify the words spoken by Miss D. within the students' individual poems.

Cooper, Susan. *King of Shadows.*
New York: Margaret K. McElderry, 1999.
This beautifully written and masterfully constructed time slip novel takes young actor Nat Fields back 400 years to the opening of the Globe Theatre.

The novel's rich visual, auditory, and olfactory descriptions will transport Readers Theatre audiences directly to the streets of Elizabethan London and the world of Shakespearean theatre. The scene in which Nat meets Will Shakespeare and first rehearses with him would translate wonderfully to a script that includes lines from *A Midsummer Night's Dream* and enables Readers Theatre actors to give a remarkable performance.

Creech, Sharon. *Love that Dog: A Novel.*
New York: Joanna Cotler/HarperCollins, 2001.
This novel in verse, composed of dated entries written in the first person from one perspective, combines Jack's responses to poems, his teacher's encouragement, the death of his dog, and his own poetry. Because there are entries that could be excerpted and still make literary sense, this single-voice novel would work as Readers Theatre without altering the precisely constructed language of the verse. For example, the entry about going to the animal shelter has lines for a father and the dog as well as for Jack. The novel is short enough that it could be read entirely in one performance, with different participants reading Jack's various entries. Different participants could read the lines Jack occasionally incorporates from other characters. Performing the whole novel would allow the audience to experience the clever evolution of the story and the beauty of the author's writing.

Curtis, Christopher Paul. *The Watsons Go to Birmingham—1963.*
New York: Delacorte, 1995.
Christopher Paul Curtis chose the first chapter of this book, the one in which Byron gets his lips frozen to the car mirror, for the 2010 ALA Readers Theatre performance in Washington, D.C. The cast had tremendous fun reading this script, and the audience enjoyed it immensely. This is an obvious choice as it introduces the Weird Watsons and their amusing family dynamics, but other chapters would also work well. For example, "Froze-Up Southern Folks," in which Kenny and Joey complain about being overdressed for the cold, is a viable choice. When Curtis was preparing his script, he appropriately eliminated much of the description and explanation. Interestingly enough, at rehearsal he commented that perhaps he had overwritten his original text. As mentioned earlier, when creating scripts, revising can become an ongoing process, even after publication. In any case, the novel's dialogue, humor, and pathos make *The Watsons Go to Bir-*

mingham—1963 ideal Readers Theatre material. Selected passages would work well as part of a presentation on the topic of civil rights.

Cushman, Karen. *The Ballad of Lucy Whipple.*
New York: Clarion, 1996.
Unhappy about being transplanted to a Gold Rush town in California, plucky, dreamy, book-loving Lucy longs to return home to Massachusetts. The chapter in which she enlists her brother's help in her pie business has the humor, fast-paced dialogue, detailed lists, and fine writing that can immediately create a winning Readers Theatre script. Sections that contain vivid descriptions of sights, sounds, and smells in and around a mining community would also make informative and effective choices.

Ellis, Deborah. *A Company of Fools.*
Toronto: Fitzhenry and Whiteside, 2002.
In the year 1348, choirboys Henri and Micah, along with a small group of monks from the Abbey of St. Luc, form a Company of Fools to sing and lighten the hearts of plague-beleaguered Parisians. Street-smart but religiously untrained Micah brings mischief, joy, and uncertainty into quiet, sickly Henri's life. The chapter in which the boys sneak off from the grand procession of monks to enjoy the Lendit Fair provides a glimpse of Paris before the plague as well as the friendship between Henri and Micah, the relationships among the other choir boys, and the personalities of some of the monks. It contains description, narration, and dialogue that could easily produce lively Readers Theatre.

Funke, Cornelia. *The Thief Lord.*
Trans. by Oliver Latsch. New York: Chicken House/Scholastic, 2002. (Originally published in Germany by Ceciline Dressler, 2000.)
Set in contemporary Venice, Italy, this exciting adventure of a gang of homeless children, a good-hearted detective, and a magical merry-go-round comes with well-drawn characters, colorful sensory details, and a satisfying ending. A number of scenes would translate well to compelling Readers Theatre, including the one in which Prosper discovers they are being followed by a detective, the one in which the gang discovers who the Thief Lord really is, and the one in which they break into Signora Spavento's home.

Hale, Shannon. *The Princess Academy.*
New York: Bloomsbury, 2005.
One of twenty mountain village girls sent to the Princess Academy to prepare for the prince's selection of his princess, feisty Mira finds a love for
learning, teaches herself the telepathic language of her homeland, helps
save the academy girls from a gang of bandits, improves her village's economic situation, and discovers her place in life. The scene in which Mira is
unfairly punished (see chapter 6), the scene in which Mira uses the "rules
of diplomacy" to rectify Tutor Olana's harsh treatment of the academy
girls, and the scene in which the bandits take the girls hostage would
make wonderful Readers Theatre. Replete with adventure, romance, and
self-discovery and growth, this smoothly crafted novel is a Readers Theatre natural.

Hobbs, Will. *Kokopelli's Flute.*
New York: Atheneum, 1995.
Life changes drastically for Tepary Jones when he blows into an ancient
bone flute left behind by pothunters in a southwestern cliff dwelling. He is
now transformed into a packrat every night. His new changeling status enables him to meet the legendary Kokopelli, find an ancient herb to cure his
mother from deadly hantavirus, bring two pothunters to justice, and trick
Coyote into staying out of his family's fields. The conversation between
packrat Tepary and wise Cricket, in which Cricket is revealed as Kokopelli,
would make a fascinating Readers Theatre presentation. Scenes in which
Tepary the packrat wreaks havoc in his home and the pothunters' camp
could be lively and offer insight into the living habits of packrats.

Holm, Jennifer L. *Our Only May Amelia.*
New York: HarperCollins, 1999.
May Amelia is the only girl in a family of Finnish homesteaders along
the Nasel River in Washington at the end of the eighteenth century. Seeing herself as a No-Good Girl, she is constantly into mischief, trying to
do what the boys do. May Amelia's forthright manner, adventure-seeking
spirit, and distinctive voice make her an extremely likeable character. Any
of her many adventures would make good Readers Theatre fare, but the
scene in which she, some brothers, and a friend encounter a cougar is
particularly exciting. The author's idiosyncratic system of capitalization

(caps are used frequently for emphasis) and punctuation (quotation marks are nonexistent) would make converting text into script an interesting and enjoyable challenge. The sequel, *The Trouble with May Amelia* (Atheneum, 2011) would also be a viable Readers Theatre choice.

Juster, Norton. *The Phantom Tollbooth.*

Illus. by Jules Feiffer. New York: Knopf, 1964. (Originally published by Epstein and Carroll, 1961.)

This entertaining allegorical tale of Milo's quest to return Princesses Rhyme and Reason to the Kingdom of Wisdom is considered a classic for readers of all ages. The exuberant plays on words and intriguing twists of logic, supplying both humor and food for thought, make for spirited Readers Theatre. Although the example given in chapter 6 uses the banquet of words scene, many scenes from *The Phantom Tollbooth* could be readily adapted into Readers Theatre scripts.

Kaaberbøl, Lene. *The Shamer's Daughter.*

London: Hodder, 2002. (Originally published in Denmark by Forlaget Forum, 2000.)

The first of four Shamer books, this is an engaging story of an eleven-year-old girl who inherits her mother's gift for seeing into people's souls and exposing their shame. Chapter 11, "Draco, Draco," which takes place in a dragon pit, would make enthralling Readers Theatre. I became acquainted with the Shamer books when Danish author Lene Kaaberbøl participated in the 2008 IBBY Readers Theatre in Copenhagen. Although not published in the United States, the Shamer books provide high-quality fantasy that is definitely worth seeking out.

McKissack, Patricia C. *Never Forgotten.*

Illus. by Leo and Diane Dillon. New York: Swartz and Wade/Random House, 2011.

Children stolen from African villages as part of the slave trade were gone but never forgotten. When Musafa was taken, Dingo the blacksmith, Musafa's widowed father, who previously invoked the assistance of Mother Elements of Earth, Fire, Water, and Wind in raising him, now enlists their help in finding him. Through their stories, Dingo learns of Musafa's abduction, his journey through the Middle Passage, and his enslavement to a Charleston blacksmith. Highly valued for his intricate work, eighth-generation blacksmith Musafa carries on his family's craft in the New World.

A picture book in verse, either the entire book or a self-contained poem, such as "The Mother Elements," would provide a stunning Readers Theatre presentation. Reading it in small Readers Theatre circles (explained in the entry on Andrea Cheng's *Where the Steps Were*), rather than to a large audience, might be an appropriate approach for this heartrending story. In either case, the opportunities for a variety of voices, the songs, and the Mother Elements' rhythmic sounds could create a moving and memorable experience for everyone involved.

Morpurgo, Michael. *War Horse.*
New York: Scholastic, 2007. (Originally published in the UK by Egmont UK, 1982.)
Beautifully written in first person from the horse's point of view, this is the story of a horse with a lot of heart, those who loved him, those who abused him, and the part he played in the Great War. Filled with warmth and pathos, the story has tremendous audience appeal. The first chapter, which sets the stage for the relationship between thirteen-year-old Albert and Joey, as he names the colt, would make exceptional Readers Theatre. Because there is so much narration from Joey, it might be advisable to have multiple readers take this role for the sake of variety. The same would apply for any passages selected for conversion.

Napoli, Donna Jo. *The Prince of the Pond.*
Illus. by Judith Byron Schachner. New York, Dutton, 1992.
Newly transformed into a frog, an enchanted prince has difficulty making his new tongue work properly. He dubs himself the Fawg Pin and goes about learning how to be a frog. However, much to the bewilderment of his frog mate, whom he calls Jade, his amphibian life is infused with human emotions and instincts. Conversations between Jade and the Fawg Pin hold potential for hilarious Readers Theatre as Jade not only translates for the Fawg, who cannot pronounce such sounds as *l, s, r,* and *th,* but also instructs him about the dynamics of mating. Designation of two narrators, one general and one associated with Jade, the deletion of speaker indicators, and assigning multiple character parts to readers are all that is needed to get this well-crafted story ready to perform.

Park, Linda Sue. *Keeping Score.*
New York: Clarion, 2008.
Maggie is passionate about baseball. She particularly loves filling out score cards using the complex system she has devised. The Korean War figures significantly in this thought-provoking novel that is set in Brooklyn in 1951 through 1954. There are many poignant passages in this multilayered coming-of-age novel. A few possibilities for Readers Theatre include the Giants vs. Dodgers game at Ebbets Field, which shell-shocked Jim fails to attend; Maggie's conversation with her father about the cause of Jim's affliction; and Maggie's discussion with Treecie about the importance of hope and trying. Linda Sue Park selected the dramatic scene in which the Dodgers lose the pennant to the Giants for the 2007 ALA Readers Theatre to perform in Washington, D.C. (See chapter 6.) She hit a home run with this one.

Paterson, Katherine. *Bread and Roses, Too.*
New York: Clarion, 2006.
This story of a 1912 labor strike is told from two perspectives: Italian immigrant schoolgirl Rosa and native-born underage mill worker Jake, and from two locations: Lawrence, Massachusetts, where the strike took place, and Barre, Vermont, where strikers' children were sent for the sake of their safety and welfare. For the 2008 IBBY Readers Theatre in Copenhagen, Katherine Paterson selected the scene in which Rosa and her mother devise the phrase "we want bread and roses, too" and Rosa creates the sign bearing this legendary slogan. (See chapter 6.) Paterson's script resulted in a moving Readers Theatre performance. Other scenes with high potential for success include the one in which Rosa's teacher, Miss Finch, visits her at her tenement flat and the one in which Jake learns about the opportunity to leave Lawrence with the strikers' children and discovers his father's dead body.

Paterson, Katherine. *The Same Stuff as Stars.*
New York: Clarion, 2002.
Angel and Bernie's father is in prison, and their feckless mother abandons them to their impoverished great-grandmother in rural Vermont. As both children form viable relationships with their feisty great-grandma, Angel gains strength and support from the mysterious star man and the sympathetic librarian. Katherine Paterson selected the chapter about the chil-

dren's introduction to Miss Liza the librarian for the 2004 IBBY Readers Theatre in Capetown. (See chapter 6.) Humor, pathos, and dialogue for three readers, along with Paterson's impeccable writing and deep sensitivity, made this a stellar Readers Theatre performance. Other likely passages include Bernie's first day at school, Angel's initial encounter with the star man, and the scene in which Angel's father tries to abduct her.

Peck, Richard. *A Year Down Yonder.*
New York: Dial, 2000.
Mary Alice has spent a week each summer with Grandma Dowdel in her small rural town in Illinois, but now, due to the recession of 1937, she lives with her for the whole school year. The more time she spends with her formidable grandmother, the more she appreciates her idiosyncratic sense of justice and unorthodox ways of making things work out as they should. The first chapter, in which Mary Alice is intimidated by a school bully, would be an excellent Readers Theatre introduction to the inimitable Grandma Dowdel. The sequel to *A Year Down Yonder, A Long Way from Chicago* (Dial, 1998) and companion novel, *A Season of Gifts* (Dial, 2009), also fraught with Mrs. Dowdel's hilarious escapades and maneuvers, would make entertaining Readers Theatre scripts as well.

Seidler, Tor. *Mean Margaret.*
Illus. by Jon Agee. New York: Laura Geringer/HarperCollins, 1997.
The orderly life of woodchuck couple Fred and Phoebe is disrupted when they discover a human baby left in the woods by its siblings because it is disagreeable and greedy. Ironically, mean and demanding Margaret ends up improving the lives of those around her, particularly her beer-guzzling human father, after she comes to appreciate the care given her by the woodchucks and their woodland friends. The chapter titled "Lousy Luck," in which the woodchucks find the child and decide to take her to their home, much to Fred's dismay, could be readily converted into a script and would be a lot of fun to perform as Readers Theatre.

Singer, Marilyn. *Central Heating: Poems About Fire and Warmth.*
Illus. by Meilo So. New York: Knopf, 2005.
The poems in this collection explore fire in its many fascinating manifestations. Marilyn Singer's exquisite free verse lends itself perfectly to Readers Theatre performances. While any of the poems in the collection

would work, the thought-provoking "Contradiction" (see chapter 6) and the humorous "Birthday Party" have high potential for warm audience appreciation.

Thor, Annika. *A Faraway Island.*
Trans. by Linda Scheneck. New York: Random House, 2009. (Originally published in Sweden by Bonnier Carlsen.)
Stephanie and her younger sister are among the five hundred Jewish children evacuated to Sweden in 1939. They are placed in separate foster homes in an island off the mainland. The anti-Semitism they experienced in Vienna at the hands of the Nazis is smoothly integrated into an appealing story focused on Stephanie's adjustment amidst difficulties in her new home and school. Although the novel contains few long scenes that would lend themselves to a sustained Readers Theatre performance, a series of brief passages could provide a memorable presentation. Possible passages include the sisters arriving in their new homes, another child unwittingly giving Stephanie a photograph of Hitler, the Easter bonfire celebration, and the arrival of the news that Germany has invaded southern Norway.

Wolff, Virginia Euwer. *The Mozart Season.*
New York: Henry Holt, 1991.
In this masterfully composed novel, twelve-year-old Allegra Shapiro is the youngest finalist in a prestigious violin competition. She spends the summer preparing Mozart's Fourth Violin Concerto. She also contemplates how the varied threads of her life—her family, her friends, her Jewish heritage, her music teacher, the dancing man, and her mother's loyal friend—intertwine with the music she plays throughout the summer. The dramatic family scene Virginia Euwer Wolff selected for the script she created for the 2007 ALA Readers Theatre in Washington, D.C., was captivating. (See chapter 6.) Some of the novel's more contemplative moments would also provide engaging Readers Theatre performances.

Wynne-Jones, Tim. *Rex Zero and the End of the World.*
New York: Melanie Kroupa/Farrar Straus Giroux, 2007. (Originally published in Canada by Groundwood, 2006.)
Rex Norton-Norton is a likeable eleven year old growing up in Canada in the early 1960s amidst the tension of the Cold War. The new kid on

the block, he helps his neighborhood friends discover the mystery of the panther. Rex's optimistic personality and offbeat sense of humor make reading from this or any of the Rex Zero novels (i.e., *Rex Zero King of Nothing,* Farrar Straus Giroux, 2008; and *Rex Zero the Great Pretender,* Farrar Straus Giroux, 2010) delightful Readers Theatre material. (See example in chapter 6.)

Books for Young Adult Audiences

Almond, David. ***Kit's Wilderness.***
New York: Delacorte, 2000. (Originally published in Great Britain by Hodder, 1999.)
Kit Watson and his family move back to his ancestral home of Stoneygate, in the north of England, to care for his elderly grandfather. The abandoned coal pits fascinate him, and he joins in a dangerous game of Death with one of the community lads. Ancient past, remembered past, present, dreams, visions, stories, drawings, and reality mysteriously swirl together in this complex, often disturbing but ultimately hopeful tale. David Almond chose the scene in which Kit plays the game of Death for the 2007 ALA Readers Theatre in Washington, D.C. (See chapter 6.) Almond's impeccable sense of pacing, keen ear for language, and incomparable storytelling ability make *Kit's Wilderness* a brilliant choice for Readers Theatre.

Almond, David. ***Skellig.***
New York: Delacorte, 1999. (Originally published in Great Britain by Hodder, 1998.)
Michael's infant sister is critically ill when his family buys a run-down house and moves across town. In the dilapidated garage, he discovers Skellig, a mysterious being who is part man, part bird, and part angel. He also finds a good friend in Mina, the home-schooled girl next door. Together, Michael and Mina help Skellig gain his strength, and Skellig in turn helps the baby survive. The novel's ample dialogue along with Almond's fine writing make this fascinating tale a natural choice for Readers Theatre. The various scenes in which Michael, Mina, and Skellig interact would easily convert to intriguing scripts. *My Name Is Mina* (Delacorte, 2011), the prequel to *Skellig,* would also make exceptional Readers Theatre.

Bartoletti, Susan Campbell. *Black Potatoes: The Story of the Great Irish Famine, 1845–1850.*
Boston: Houghton Mifflin, 2001.
This comprehensive look at the Great Irish Famine provides an abundance of detail on one of Europe's great tragedies. Historical background on the enmity between England and Ireland, Protestants and Irish Catholics, and the wealthy and the poor sheds light on the conflict that evolved when the potato crops failed and the people of Ireland went hungry. The clarity and fluidity of Susan Campbell Bartoletti's writing, the detailed information about life and politics during the famine, and the insight into the effects of sustained hardship could create compelling Readers Theatre with the potential for deepening people's empathy for the Irish then and now. (See chapter 6 for script suggestions.)

Billingsley, Franny. *Chime.*
New York: Dial, 2011.
The novel begins with Briony confessing to being a witch and requesting that she be hanged. Then follows the story that leads to her trial and the shocking truth. Not your typical witchcraft trial story, this is a mystery, a romance, a character study, and a foray into the lore of the Old Ones. The opening scene would make spellbinding Readers Theatre and entice the audience to read this masterfully written fantasy. An audience familiar with the book might appreciate hearing the scene near the end of the book in which the ghosts reveal their side of the story. In any case, *Chime* rings with potential for dramatic Readers Theatre.

Cheng, Andrea. *Brushing Mom's Hair.*
Illus. by Nicole Wong. Honesdale, PA: Wordsong, 2009.
Fifty-three short poems quietly convey Ann's experiences as her mother undergoes treatment for breast cancer. Many of the poems are self-contained enough to be read individually. A sequence could be selected that provides the gist of the story line, but the complete novel in verse is compact enough to be read in its entirety as one powerful Readers Theatre performance. (See chapter 6 for suggestions.)

Engle, Margarita. *The Firefly Letters.*
New York: Henry Holt, 2010.
Using the voices of four characters, this masterfully executed novel in verse tells the story of a Swedish suffragette's three-month visit to Cuba in

1851. The novel is short enough to read completely, either to a large audience or in small Readers Theatre circles for the benefit of the four readers and perhaps a few guests. Several sections could stand alone as a Readers Theatre performance. One of these begins with Cecelia describing how the women and children use fireflies for their own amusement and ends with Cecelia and Fredrika buying the fireflies to set them free. In the middle of all this, Fredrika discovers the horridness of the Cuban slave trade. Another self-contained section tells of the time Fredrika and Cecelia spent in a simple home in the Cuban countryside and the impressions they formed.

Hesse, Karen. *Out of the Dust: A Novel.*
New York: Scholastic, 1997.
Set in Oklahoma during the Great Depression, this exquisitely rendered novel in verse is the harrowing story of fourteen-year-old Billie Jo. As one dream or another turns to dust and blows away, Billie Jo records her observations, feelings, and questions in poignant free verse. Numerous passages in this novel would make outstanding Readers Theatre while also providing insight into a deeply distressing period in American history. Although all the poems are told from Billie Jo's perspective, quite a few, such as "Rules of Dining," "Debts," and "Give Up on Wheat," have Ma and Daddy as speakers and could easily be converted to scripts for three or perhaps four readers. Others, such as "Our Path of Sorrow," could be modified to be read by three or more readers. (See chapter 6 for an example.) But whether one poem or a sequence of poems is selected, the eloquence of the Hesse's free verse will translate naturally and beautifully into powerful Readers Theatre.

Hoffman, Mary. *The Falconer's Knot: A Story of Friars, Flirtation and Foul Play.*
New York: Bloomsbury, 2007. (Originally published in Great Britain by Bloomsbury, 2007.)
Murder, intrigue, romance! Set in an Italian friary and convent, this medieval mystery would make exciting Readers Theatre. Falsely accused of murder, nobleman's son Silvano is given sanctuary in a Franciscan friary. As a young woman without a dowry, Chiara is forced by her brother to join the Poor Clares in the adjacent convent. Both newcomers grind pigments for artists who create basilica frescoes in nearby Assisi. A string of murders in the friary causes their paths to cross in interesting and unusual ways. The scene in which Silvano first accompanies Brother Anselmo to Assisi, which

includes lots of dialogue as well as necessary information for the ensuing plot, would make a first-rate Readers Theatre script.

McCaughrean, Geraldine. *The White Darkness.*
New York: HarperTempest, 2007. (Originally published in Great Britain by Oxford University Press, 2005.)
Fourteen-year-old Symone has been raised to love Antarctica, but the idea of falling in love with the long-dead Captain "Titus" Oates, from Scott's 1911 expedition to the South Pole, and making him her imaginary companion stems entirely from her own highly developed imagination. Although ecstatic when her uncle Victor takes her on their own Antarctic expedition, she worries that her mum does not know their whereabouts. Fortunately, she has Titus with her when the journey turns hellish and her life hangs on one frozen thread after another. This fast-paced Antarctic wilderness survival adventure would make chillingly delicious Readers Theatre. The early section, in which Symone's fellow travelers are introduced, would be interesting and entertaining. The middle chapter, "A Slight Change of Plan," in which the plot thickens as Uncle Victor's obsession is revealed, could captivate audience members and entice them to read the entire book.

Mora, Pat. *Dizzy in Your Eyes: Poems About Love.*
New York: Knopf, 2010.
This gem of a collection contains numerous poems that, although written for a single voice, can easily be read by more than one reader. (See chapter 6.) However, one poem, "Conversation/Conversatión," already written for two speakers, would need nothing more than two readers eager to read a bilingual poem as part of a Readers Theatre performance. The theme of love, explored in its various manifestations, adds to the collection's appeal.

Myers, Walter Dean. *Lockdown.*
New York: Amistad/HarperCollins, 2010.
Fourteen-year-old Reese is serving a two-year sentence in Progress juvenile facility for stealing prescription pads and selling them to a drug dealer. He could easily get sucked into the criminal scene for life unless he learns how to sidestep trouble, both in juvy jail and when he returns to the streets of New York. Chapters 5 and 6, which paint a vivid picture of

Reese's tough life in Progress, would make gripping Readers Theatre. The quick-paced dialogue, written in an honest, straightforward style, could be readily converted into a compelling script, and Reese's contemplation of his precarious situation could provide ample food for thought.

Myers, Walter Dean. *145th Street: Short Stories.*
New York: Delacorte, 2000.
Walter Dean Myers transports readers to contemporary Harlem via ten carefully wrought short stories. The subject matter of individual stories ranges from illegal drugs and gang violence to premonitions of death, but the undergirding element of enduring love and support from family, friends, and community connects all ten stories. Self-contained plots, swift-paced action, and abundant quantities of slang-infused dialogue make any of the stories excellent candidates for Readers Theatre. Walter Dean Myers once selected "The Baddest Dog in Harlem" for a highly successful Readers Theatre performance in which he participated. Stories from this collection could be used in an author-centered Readers Theatre, along with poetry, fiction, or nonfiction written by Myers, or in conjunction with selections for theme-based performances.

Nye, Naomi Shihab. *Habibi.*
New York: Simon and Schuster, 1997.
Liyana's father was born in Palestine and her mother was born in America; her family is Arab-American. When she is fourteen, her family moves from their home in Kansas City, Missouri, to a small village near Jerusalem. With her spiritual but nontraditional religious upbringing, Liyana is open to new experiences and the possibility of peace in a troubled world. Her friendship with a Jewish boy causes even her open-minded father to express temporary concern. A timeless story, Liyana's heartfelt contemplations, and Naomi Shihab Nye's poetical writing combine to make this enduring novel an excellent candidate for Readers Theatre. The chapter titled "To the Village" could be converted into a lively script that would acquaint audience members with both the landscape of the West Bank as well as Liyana's large extended family. The beautifully written "Twenty-ninth Day of School" would also make superb Readers Theatre material.

Wolff, Virginia Euwer. *Make Lemonade.*
New York: Henry Holt, 1993.
LaVaughn, fourteen and wanting to earn money for college, accepts a job babysitting for Jolly, a seventeen-year-old single mother of two. The difficulty of Jolly's life steels LaVaughn's resolve to escape the poverty in which she lives. With LaVaughn's help, Jolly eventually returns to school. The girls' mutually beneficial friendship, movingly depicted in Virginia Euwer Wolff's masterful novel in verse, has great potential for Readers Theatre. Sequences 38 through 43, in which LaVaughn helps Jolly return to school, would work particularly well. The example in chapter 6 from *This Full House,* the third novel in Wolff's Make Lemonade trilogy, shows how lines can be assigned to multiple readers even though the story is told from LaVaughn's perspective.

Wynne-Jones, Tim. *A Thief in the House of Memory.*
New York: Farrar Straus Giroux, 2005. (Originally published in Canada by Groundwood, 2004.)
Suspense and questions about Declan's mother, who disappeared six years ago but now seems to reappear in the memory-filled mansion where she used to live, make this an intriguing read. But it is the exceptionally smooth writing that makes this novel a natural choice for Readers Theatre. The chapter titled "I-Less," which introduces us to Dec's geeky friends, would be fun to perform. Chapters selected from the beginning, middle, and end of the novel would whet the audience's appetite for this well-wrought mystery.

Sample Program

AS NOTED IN CHAPTER 5, I ALWAYS PROVIDE THE AUDIENCE WITH A PRO-
gram that not only indicates the order of the readings and provides bios
of the performers, but also includes information about Readers Theatre.
The program is modeled after the playbill booklets given at professional
theatre productions. Here is the program I developed for the 2008 IBBY
Readers Theatre given in Copenhagen.

Readers Theatre as an International Experience

Performed by
Louis Jensen, Lene Kaaberbøl, Katherine Paterson, Peter Sís

Organized by Elizabeth Poe

Program
Performance

> *Bread and Roses, Too* by Katherine Paterson
> *Skeleton on Wheels* by Louis Jensen (Translated by Joan Tale)
> *Shadowgate* by Lene Kaaberbøl (Translated by Don Bartlett)
> *The Wall: Growing Up Behind the Iron Curtain* by Peter Sís
> Practical Applications

Creating Readers Theatre *by Elizabeth Poe*

Q & A

A Behind the Scenes Look at Readers Theatre
by Elizabeth Poe and the 2008 IBBY Readers Theatre Troupe

Who's Who in the Cast

Louis Jensen, who is featured in the most recent issue of *Bookbird,* is heralded as "one of the most established writers for children in Denmark." Since his first children's book, *Krystalmanden (The Crystal Man)* was published in 1986, he has written novels, short stories, and a play. His collections of hundreds of short "square" prose stories, the first of which is titled *Hundrede Historier (A Hundred Stories),* is a project that has brought him great notoriety. Today marks his debut performance in Readers Theatre. He lives in Århus, Denmark.

Lene Kaaberbøl published her first book when she was fifteen years of age and has been a prolific author ever since. Her books include the *Shamer Quartet,* the *W.I.T.C.H.* series (for which she won a Mickey Award for Best Disney Novel Writer of the Year), the *Katriona* Trilogy, the *Christian* series, the *Broken Orb* books, *The Morning Land,* and *Shadowgate,* an IBBY Honor Book. She has worked as a high school teacher, a copy editor, a publishing editor, and a riding teacher. Although she has a background in theatre, this is her first foray into Readers Theatre. She lives in Frederiksberg, Denmark. Her website address is www.kaaberboel.dk.

Katherine Paterson was awarded both the Hans Christian Andersen and the Astrid Lindgren Awards. She received Newbery Medals for *The Bridge to Terabithia,* which also received a Silver Pencil Award from the Netherlands and the Janusz Korczak Medal from Poland, and *Jacob Have I Loved.* In addition to *Bread and Roses, Too,* she has written *The Same Stuff as Stars; Preacher's Boy; Jip, His Story,* which won the Scott O'Dell Award for Historical Fiction; *Flip-Flop Girl; Lyddie,* which was an IBBY Honor Book; *The Tale of the Mandarin Ducks,* winner of the Boston Globe/Horn Book Picture Book Award; *Park's Quest; The Tongue-Cut Sparrow; Come Sing Jimmy Jo; Rebels of the Heavenly Kingdom; The Great Gilly Hopkins,* winner of the National Book Award and a Newbery Honor Award; *The Master Puppeteer,* which won a National Book Award and an Edgar Allan Poe Special Award; and *Of Nightingales that Weep,* a Phoenix Award winner. Katherine has appeared in a variety of Readers Theatre productions across the United States as well as the 2004 IBBY Readers Theatre in South Africa. She lives in Barre, Vermont, and her website is www.terabithia.com.

Peter Sís is a MacArthur Fellow, an honor affectionately referred to as "winning a Genius Award." He has received Caldecott Honors for *Starry Messenger: Galileo Galilei, Tibet Through the Red Box,* and *The Wall: Growing Up Behind the Iron Curtain,* which also received a Sibert Award. A six-time winner of the New York Times Book Review Best Illustrated Book of the Year, he is also the winner of a Society of Illustrators Gold Award for *Komodo.* His illustrations have appeared in *Time* Magazine, *The Atlantic Monthly, Newsweek,* and *Esquire.* He has designed many book jackets and posters; his public art graces airports and subway stations. Although he is an acclaimed filmmaker, he is new to Readers Theatre. Born in Czechoslovakia, he now resides in New York City. His website is www.petersis.com.

Elizabeth Poe, retired professor of children's literature, young adult literature, and English education, is a former editor of NCTE's *Journal of Children's Literature* and IRA's *SIGNAL Journal.* A member of the 2007 Caldecott Committee, she currently serves on the USBBY Outstanding International Books Committee and chairs the ALSC International Relations Committee. She has conducted numerous Readers Theatre workshops for students and organized Readers Theatre performances with authors at IRA and ALA conferences across the United States and at IBBY world congresses in South Africa and Denmark. She lives in Morgantown, West Virginia.

Sample Readers Theatre Classroom Assignment

BECAUSE READERS THEATRE IS A CREATIVE ENDEAVOR AND THUS DIFFI-cult to grade, teachers and librarians in school settings may be reluctant to make it an assignment. Faced with this dilemma, students in one of my English education methods courses devised the following assignment and grading rubric. I have used it frequently in Readers Theatre workshops and offer it here as an example. (The accompanying handout mentioned is an abbreviated version of information covered in chapters 1 through 5 of this text.)

Readers Theatre Assignment

Work with your group over one week to write a script for your Readers Theatre. Select a scene that can be performed in about five to ten minutes. The scene should be dramatically moving, a reading motivator, or something memorable. Each group member must have a speaking role, and the group must practice the script together in order to familiarize themselves with their parts, both words and limited actions. Please use the suggestions provided on the accompanying handout.

On the day of the performance, each group will turn in a copy of the script that includes:

- The book title and page numbers
- Group name and each member's name
- Each member's role

Readers Theatre Scoring Rubric

GROUP NAME: _____

SCRIPT

Selection of important and appropriate material   _____ /15

Book title, page numbers, group name,
members' names, and roles   _____ /10

                                              Subtotal _____ /25

PERFORMANCE

5–10 minutes in length   _____ /5

Everyone has a speaking part   _____ /5

Rehearsal is evident   _____ /5

Actors enjoy themselves   _____ /5

Text is most important component   _____ /5

                                              Subtotal _____ /25

                                              TOTAL _____ /50

Handout created by Dr. Poe and her English education students:
Denise Cyphers, Julie Kidd, and Sarah Marsh

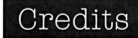

Credits

CHAPTER 1

1. From *A Kitten Tale* by Eric Rohmann, copyright © 2008 by Eric Rohmann. Used by permission of Alfred A. Knopf, an imprint of Random House Children's Books, a division of Random House, Inc.

CHAPTER 6

1. Excerpt from *Wild About Books* by Judy Sierra and Marc Brown, copyright © 2004 by Judy Sierra. Illustrations copyright © 2004 by Marc Brown. Used by permission of Random House Children's Books, a division of Random House, Inc.

2. Excerpt from *Bubble Trouble* by Margaret Mahy, illustrated by Polly Dunbar. Text copyright © 2008 by Margaret Mahy. Reprinted by permission of Clarion Books, an imprint of Houghton Mifflin Harcourt Publishing Company.

3. Excerpt from *Mike Mulligan and His Steam Shovel* by Virginia Lee Burton. Copyright © 1939 by Virginia Lee Burton, © renewed

1967 by Virginia Lee Demetrios. Reprinted by permission of Houghton Mifflin Harcourt Publishing Company. All rights reserved.

4. From *Marvin One Too Many* by Katherine Paterson. Harper Collins © 2001 Minna Murra, Inc.

5. Excerpt from *Rex Zero and the End of the World* by Tim Wynne-Jones, copyright © 2007 by Tim Wynne-Jones. Reprinted by permission of Farrar, Straus and Giroux.

6. From *Brushing Mom's Hair* by Andrea Cheng. Copyright © 2009 by Andrea Cheng. Published by Boyds Mills Press. Reprinted by permission.

7. "October," from *Tap Dancing on the Roof: Sijo (poems)* by Linda Sue Park. Text copyright © 2007 by Linda Sue Park. Reprinted by permission of Clarion Books, an imprint of Houghton Mifflin Harcourt Publishing Company.

8. "I Can Dance," from *Dizzy in Your Eyes: Poems About Love* by Pat Mora, copyright © 2010 by Pat Mora. Used by permission of Alfred A. Knopf, an imprint of Random House Children's Books, a division of Random House, Inc.

9. "Contradiction," from *Central Heating: Poems About Fire and Warmth* by Marilyn Singer, copyright © 2005 by Marilyn Singer. Used by permission of Alfred A. Knopf, an imprint of Random House Children's Books, a division of Random House, Inc.

10. "Shotgun Cheatham's Last Night Above Ground," by Richard Peck, from *Twelve Shots: Outstanding Short Stories about Guns*, edited by Harry Mazer. Copyright © 1997 by Richard Peck. Reprinted by permission of Random House, Inc.

11. Excerpt from *The Wall* by Peter Sís. Copyright © 2007 by Peter Sís. Reprinted by permission of Farrar, Straus and Giroux, LLC.

Index

CPSIA information can be obtained at www.ICGtesting.com
Printed in the USA
LVOW05s1201260114

371017LV00019B/1015/P